CONTENTS

	PROLOGUE: "The Times That Try Women's Souls"	1
1	A Quaker Girlhood	5
2	The Financial Crisis	20
3	An Unconventional Young Woman	32
4	All the Good You Can	45
5	A Nation in Need of Reform	57
6	Civil War	77
7	Emancipation	96
8	We the People	109
9	Betrayal	126
10	Let the World Wag	148
11	A New Generation	168
12	Afterward	191
13	Legacy	193

NOTES...200
TIME LINE..216
SELECTED WRITINGS
OF SUSAN B. ANTHONY..............................219
BIBLIOGRAPHY.......................................224
ACKNOWLEDGMENTS................................229
INDEX..230

Susan B. Anthony, 1855

PRAISE FOR
THE MAKING OF AMERICA

ALEXANDER HAMILTON

"Kanefield is a capable nonfiction writer, organizing an eloquent review of Hamilton's life . . . the story is told easily, making a founding father accessible to young readers the same way Lin-Manuel Miranda has done on Broadway."
—*Voices of Youth Advocates (VOYA)*

ANDREW JACKSON

★ "This book is an eye-opening, accurately researched, well-written depiction of Andrew Jackson and his presidency. Kanefield does an excellent job of describing Jackson's qualities as a leader—both good and bad."
—*School Library Connection, starred review*

ABRAHAM LINCOLN

"This concise and balanced narrative encapsulates the life and legacy of one of the country's most important leaders . . . A solid addition for understanding America's story."
—*Kirkus Reviews*

SUSAN B. ANTHONY

"Susan B. Anthony, who fought tirelessly for women to have the right to vote, is profiled in this very readable entry in the Making of America series."
—*Booklist*

> There is properly no history,
> only biography.
> —*Ralph Waldo Emerson*

★ ★ ★ ★ ★ ★ ★ ★ ★ ★ ★ ★ ★ ★ ★

The Making of America series traces the constitutional history of the United States through overlapping biographies of American men and women. The debates that raged when our nation was founded have been argued ever since: *How should the Constitution be interpreted? What is the meaning, and where are the limits, of personal liberty? What is the proper role of the federal government? Who should be included in "we the people"?* Each biography in the series tells the story of an American leader who helped shape the United States of today.

THE MAKING OF AMERICA
SUSAN B. ANTHONY

★ TERI KANEFIELD ★

✶ ✶ ✶ ✶ ✶ ✶ ✶ ✶

All images used in this book are public domain with the following exception:

Page 199: Reuters/Adam Fenste.

Cataloging-in-Publication Data has been applied for
and may be obtained from the Library of Congress.

Paperback ISBN 978-1-4197-4576-8

Text copyright © 2019 Teri Kanefield

Book design by Sara Corbett

Published in paperback in 2020 by Abrams Books for Young Readers, an imprint of ABRAMS. Originally published in hardcover by Abrams Books for Young Readers in 2019. All rights reserved. No portion of this book may be reproduced, stored in a retrieval system, or transmitted in any form or by any means, mechanical, electronic, photocopying, recording, or otherwise, without written permission from the publisher.

Printed and bound in U.S.A.

10 9 8 7 6 5 4 3 2 1

Abrams Books for Young Readers are available at special discounts when purchased in quantity for premiums and promotions as well as fundraising or educational use. Special editions can also be created to specification. For details, contact specialsales@abramsbooks.com or the address below.

Abrams® and The Making of America® are registered
trademarks of Harry N. Abrams, Inc.

ABRAMS The Art of Books
195 Broadway, New York, NY 10007
abramsbooks.com

★ PROLOGUE ★

"The Times That Try Women's Souls"

The year was 1856, and Susan B. Anthony, thirty-five years old, was traveling through upstate New York with a friend and fellow activist, Frances Gage. They were on a speaking tour to talk to women about their rights, and to speak against slavery. It was January and bitterly cold. When their sleigh emerged from a line of snowdrifts, they found themselves at a small country inn where they would stay for the night. Soon they were warming themselves by the fire.

The wife of the innkeeper was young, still in her teens, with a baby fifteen months old. When Anthony and Gage arrived, the

SUSAN B. ANTHONY

supper dishes were piled in the sink and the baby was crying. But the young wife rose to the occasion. While she prepared supper for her guests, she also rocked the baby to sleep and washed the dishes. While the wife worked, her husband sat in the barroom with a group of men, talking. He did nothing to help her. In a corner was a rack where the ironing was done: baby dresses, embroidered petticoats, men's shirts. Anthony knew every item of clothing had been produced by the woman's own hands.

Before long, the wife had laid out a fine meal: white bread, butter, cheese, pickles, apple and mince pie, and peach preserves. Anthony had made a special request, which was also on the table: baked apples and a glass of milk. After Anthony and Gage finished their supper, the wife showed them to a bedroom already warmed for them.

The next day, when it was time to pay the bill, the husband appeared. He took the money and slipped it into his pocket. The law, Anthony knew, "gives him the right to every dollar [his wife] earns, and when she needs two cents to buy a darning needle, she has to ask him and explain what she wants it for." Anthony bristled at the injustice.

The story repeated itself at another tavern. This time, the innkeeper's wife had a baby sick with whooping cough. The wife

"The Times That Try Women's Souls"

scrambled to get dinner for her boarders. The husband stood with his hands in his pockets, watching. At one point the wife begged her husband to take the baby for ten minutes. He took the child, but before ten minutes were up, he handed the baby back saying, "Here, take this child, I'm tired."

The next day, when the time came to pay the bill, the husband was on hand to receive the money. Anthony had no choice but to give it to him, even though doing so broke her heart. "Well good folks at home," Anthony concluded the story in a letter, "these surely are the times that try women's souls."

Anthony knew that such incidents weren't the worst. The law allowed a man to beat his wife. It was almost impossible for a woman to obtain a divorce, and even those who could found themselves blocked from almost all professions and hence unable to support themselves. While an unmarried woman had some rights—she could hold property in her own name, for example— once a woman was married, she lost her separate legal identity under law of *coverture*, a word that literally means "to protect" or "to cover."

Under the law of coverture, husband and wife were considered a single entity, with the husband possessing total control and authority over his wife and her possessions. A married woman could not enter into contracts, apply for credit, own real estate or personal property in her own name, or even obtain an education without her husband's permission. Any children of the marriage were under the sole guardianship of the husband. As Anthony saw the situation, "Women's subsistence is in the hands of men, and most arbitrarily and unjustly does he exercise his consequent power."

Susan B. Anthony was on a quest for justice. With the rallying cry of "Men their rights, nothing more; women their rights, nothing less," she intended to end the oppression of women in America.

1
A Quaker Girlhood

*"I doubt if there be any mortal who clings
to loves with greater tenacity than do I."*
—*Susan B. Anthony*

Susan Brownell Anthony was born on February 15, 1820, in the lush, rolling foothills of the Berkshires, about a mile from the village of Adams, Massachusetts. It was a place where winters were long and brutal, and summers short. Still heavily influenced by the Puritan settlers who founded the colony of Massachusetts, Adams was a place where self-discipline and hard work were admired, and frivolity was widely frowned upon.

When Susan's grandparents settled in the foothills of the

★ ★ ★ ★ ★ ★ SUSAN B. ANTHONY ★ ★ ★ ★ ★ ★

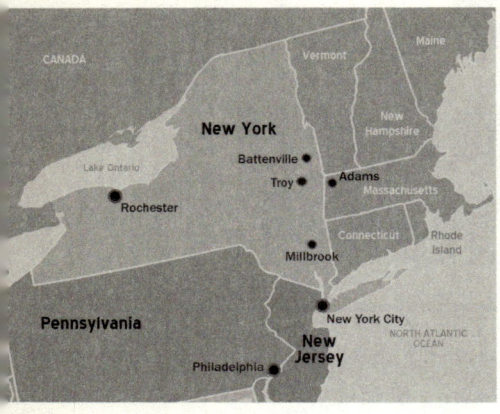

Map showing towns of importance in Anthony's early life

Berkshires, Adams was a remote frontier town, and little was known of what lay westward beyond the mountains. Susan's maternal grandfather fought in the Revolutionary War. He enlisted immediately after the first shots were fired at Lexington, when the entire colony was ablaze with enthusiasm for American independence. He served with distinction, and afterward was elected to the Massachusetts legislature. He acquired large tracts of land near Adams and prospered.

Birthplace of Susan B. Anthony. Photograph taken in 1897. Susan was born in the room shaded by the tree. The windows had been replaced since Susan's birth—otherwise, the house was the same.

A Quaker Girlhood

Susan's parents, Lucy Read and Daniel Anthony, grew up on neighboring farms. Daniel's family were members of the Religious Society of Friends, also called Quakers because they were said to tremble in the sight of the Lord. Quakers lived an austere life without music or frills so they could dedicate themselves to God. Their religious gatherings were called meetings, and their places of worship were called meetinghouses.

> Quakers originated in England, where they were persecuted for their beliefs, including the notion—considered radical at the time—that all people were equal. This belief in perfect equality put them at odds with the social order in England, which placed lords and royalty above common people. They came to America to avoid persecution, where they became social reformers. They were among the first abolitionists, and later worked to end racial segregation.

Lucy, while descended from Puritans, was raised in a more relaxed household. She was allowed to wear brightly colored clothing, dance at parties, and sing as she worked at her spinning wheel. As children, Lucy and Daniel attended school together in the one-room schoolhouse Daniel's father had built on his property. Elsewhere in America, debates were raging over whether girls should be educated, but Quakers, with their belief that all people were equal in the sight of God, educated their daughters alongside their sons. Women were even allowed to speak at Quaker meetings.

Lucy and Daniel's sisters were close friends, and Daniel was "the torment of their lives," jumping out at them unexpectedly, eavesdropping to learn their secrets, and generally annoying them "in ways common to boys of all generations." At the age of nineteen, Daniel set off for a newly established Quaker boarding school in Millbrook, New York. He returned a few years later to find that Lucy had blossomed into the prettiest girl in the village. Daniel declared his love and asked her to marry him.

There were two obstacles. The first was that the Quakers in Adams had a strict rule: Members were not allowed to marry non-Quakers. The second was that Lucy didn't know if she *wanted* to marry a Quaker. She had a lovely singing voice and she wasn't sure she wanted to give up music, singing, and pretty clothes. Love won out. She agreed to marry Daniel—but she wanted to attend one last party. On July 9, 1817, Daniel sat stiffly against the wall at

A Quaker Girlhood

the party wearing his black broad-brimmed hat, waiting patiently until four in the morning, when at last Lucy had danced to her heart's content. Four days later, they were married.

The Quaker elders, shocked and angry, promptly excluded Daniel from the group. Daniel responded by saying, "I am sorry that in order to marry the woman I love best, I had to violate a rule of the religious society I revered the most." He asked to be allowed back. The Quakers weighed the matter and found Daniel otherwise a devoted and sincere Quaker, so they let him return. Lucy's impression was that Daniel told his fellow Quakers that he was sorry he had married her, and she resented it. Lucy attended Quaker meetings with her husband, but she refused to become

Daniel Anthony and Lucy Read Anthony, parents of Susan B. Anthony. Photographer and date unknown.

a Quaker herself, insisting that she wasn't "good" enough. She thus defied the Quakers twice, first by marrying Daniel, then by refusing to convert.

When Susan learned the story of her parents' marriage, her admiration for both of them grew. She thought the story terribly romantic, and she felt proud that her parents were not afraid to defy expectations or risk losing the good opinion of their neighbors to do what each thought was right.

✷ ✷ ✷ ✷ ✷ ✷ ✷ ✷ ✷ ✷ ✷ ✷ ✷ ✷ ✷

Lucy's parents gave the newlyweds a tract of land for their new home. Daniel built a house in the Quaker style: large and sturdy, but without frills and decorations. Their first child, Guelma, was born the year after they were married. Seventeen months later, Susan was born, and the year after that came a third girl named Hannah.

When the time came for Lucy to give birth a fourth time, Susan and her sisters stayed with their paternal grandparents. Susan was three years old. She and her sisters remained with their grandparents for six weeks. The teacher employed at their grandfather's school shared books with Guelma and Susan and taught them to spell and read. Susan was proud of her new skill.

A Quaker Girlhood

While at her grandparents' house, Susan and her sisters also suffered through a bout of whooping cough.

Meanwhile, at home, tragedy struck: Lucy's fourth baby was born dead. After Susan and her sisters returned home, Lucy noticed that Susan's eyes had become crossed. Lucy believed that the strain of reading while recovering from whooping cough caused the problem. In time Susan's left eye straightened out, but her right eye remained slightly crossed with a tendency to wander—a disability that made reading difficult all her life.

✱ ✱ ✱ ✱ ✱ ✱ ✱ ✱ ✱ ✱ ✱ ✱ ✱ ✱ ✱

Susan was still a toddler when her father gave up farming to enter the nation's new cotton industry. He built a factory three stories high with twenty-six looms next to the brook that flowed through Lucy's parents' property. The rippling water turned an overshot wheel, twenty-six feet in diameter, which in turn powered the looms.

Like other factory owners throughout New England, Daniel hired girls, usually between the ages of thirteen and eighteen, to work the looms. The young women were mostly from the poorest rural areas. They toiled in the factory from six in the morning until six at night with Sundays off. It was customary for millworkers to board in the homes of the factory owners, so the house of Susan's girlhood was bustling with activity. Daniel established an evening school and taught his millworkers to read and write. Initially, Daniel taught the classes himself; later, he hired professional teachers.

While the Quakers believed that men and women were spiritual equals, in Quaker households, as elsewhere, tending to the home and children was women's work. Lucy prepared meals for her family plus eleven millworkers, cooking on the open hearth in a big kitchen fireplace, baking bread in a brick oven. She also made and cared for everyone's clothing, including the millworkers'. Because the factory produced cotton cloth, she didn't have to spin the thread or weave the fabric herself, but she did the sewing, washing, and ironing.

Susan was four years old when Lucy gave birth to another child, named Daniel Jr. for his father. As soon as Susan and her sisters were able to, they performed household chores to help their mother. Susan, Guelma, and Hannah spent entire days baking bread. By the age of ten, Susan could cook a meal for the entire household. The mill was prosperous enough so that there would have been enough money to hire servants, but New Englanders valued hard work. With the exception of a

A Quaker Girlhood

thirteen-year-old girl who was paid to help Lucy for a few hours each day, Lucy never considered hiring household servants.

Daniel Sr. traveled often, regularly journeying forty miles to Troy, New York, where he purchased wagonloads of cotton. Dressed smartly in his black suit and hat, he even traveled as far as New York City and Philadelphia to visit banks and take care of business. Most days Lucy didn't venture farther than the spring where she drew water. Lucy grew careworn, inward, and quiet. She rarely spoke of her feelings, but Susan sensed she was unhappy. It was hard for Susan to imagine her mother as the fun-loving, dancing, and singing young girl she had once been.

In keeping with the Quaker belief that toys and games distracted from what the Quakers called the "Inner Light,"—the bit of God inside each of us—there were very few toys in the house. When Susan and her sisters were freed from their chores, their parents encouraged them to play outdoors. Susan and her sisters roamed the hills. In summer, they picked wildflowers. In winter, they played in the snow, or in the attic.

Susan was the most outspoken of the Anthony girls—a trait her parents accepted, and even encouraged. Once, after Lucy chided Susan for stopping at her grandmother's house instead of coming directly home for dinner, Susan said, "Grandma's

SUSAN B. ANTHONY

potato peelings are better than your boiled dinners!" Her mother shrugged it off as an example of Susan's tartness.

✦ ✦ ✦ ✦ ✦ ✦ ✦ ✦ ✦ ✦ ✦ ✦ ✦ ✦ ✦

After Daniel successfully operated his mill for three years, he received a business offer from John McLean of Battenville, New York, a former judge and the owner of a larger mill on the banks of the swiftly flowing Batten Kill River. McLean offered to put up the money to get his mill working if Daniel would bring his operating skills. Daniel, ambitious and enterprising, couldn't resist, so the Anthonys made plans to move to Battenville, forty-five miles away.

On a bright July morning in 1826, the judge himself came to fetch the Anthonys in a large green wagon pulled by two fine horses. They made the journey in a single day. Their household possessions came later in humbler wagons. Until they could move into a house of their own, they lived in the McLean mansion, where Susan and her sisters saw people of African descent for the first time—an enslaved mother and her daughter named Sue who toiled in the McLeans' household. Susan took a liking to Sue and befriended her. Hannah, frightened, shied away. Daniel seized the opportunity to explain to his children the horrors of slavery and how children like Sue could be sold away from their parents and never see them again.

Daniel constructed a temporary home for his family until he could build a larger, permanent house. Susan and her sisters attended a local school. The schoolmaster refused to teach Susan long division because she was a girl, so Susan taught herself. Daniel, proud of Susan's ability to learn long division and her pluckiness in teaching herself, took his children out of the local school and established a private home school. He invited other children in the neighborhood to attend.

The year after they moved to Battenville, Lucy gave birth to another child, a girl named Mary, bringing the number of children up to five, four girls and a boy. Meanwhile, the factory prospered. Daniel bought mills and factories in nearby towns and hired more workers. Susan's curiosity often lured her into the Battenville factory, where she stood watching the whirring of the looms and the nimble fingers of the millworkers. The overseer was a man named Elijah. Susan noticed that whenever one of the looms malfunctioned or the yarn became tangled on the loom, Elijah called on Sally Ann Hyatt, one of the weavers, to fix the problem. "I'll tend your loom," he always said to Sally Ann, "if you'll look after this." Sally Ann quickly and expertly resolved the problem.

Susan, who was then eleven years old, asked her father, "If Sally Ann knows more about weaving than Elijah, then why don't you make her overseer?"

"It would never do," Daniel Anthony told his daughter, "to have a woman overseer in the mill."

His answer surprised and disappointed Susan. One day, Sally Ann fell ill and couldn't work. Both Susan and Hannah begged to be allowed to take her place at the mill. They drew straws and Susan was the winner. For the entire two weeks Sally Ann was in bed recovering, Susan worked as a spooler—and she experienced the pleasure of having money of her own. She gave half of her earnings to Hannah, who bought a pretty green bead bag. Susan spent the rest on china cups, which she gave her mother as a gift.

The following year, Lucy gave birth to another girl named Eliza. That same year, the family's permanent home was completed and they moved in. Susan, now thirteen, was considered old enough to become a governing member of the Society of Friends. She was eager to be counted among the leaders. She loved Quaker meetings, which were unstructured, with long silences, punctuated by members speaking about issues of importance to the community. Susan, an earnest child, admired the Quaker values of integrity, equality, and simplicity.

A Quaker Girlhood

✴ ✴ ✴ ✴ ✴ ✴ ✴ ✴ ✴ ✴ ✴ ✴ ✴ ✴ ✴ ✴

Lucy gave birth to her last child on April 19, 1834—a boy named Jacob Merritt. Two months later, two-year-old Eliza died of scarlet fever.

Despite the deaths of two siblings and her constant fear that her mother was overworked, Susan later looked back on her childhood as a happy one. Lucy, remembering the fun and laughter from her own childhood, allowed her daughters to attend parties. Susan, though, wasn't interested in boys. "I was much too serious," she said. "And I am sure they were not interested in me. Why, I wouldn't have left my book for one of them . . . when I got well into my teens and used to go to parties with my sisters, my mother would commission me to act as dragon and drag the others home. And I never failed her."

As teenagers, Susan, Guelma, and Hannah took jobs teaching young children of prominent families, positions that often included the duties of a nanny. Ordinarily only the poorest girls worked outside the home, but Daniel and Lucy wanted their girls to learn to be independent. Of the few occupations open to women—factory work, domestic service, teaching, and sewing—teaching earned the most respect because it required an education, something few women possessed in the early part of the nineteenth century. To be able to advance in the profession beyond teaching young children, though, Daniel's daughters would need more education than he could provide at home. Daniel therefore chose Deborah Moulson's Female Seminary in Hamilton, Pennsylvania, not far from Philadelphia.

Guelma, the oldest, was the first to go, leaving home to attend the seminary in 1836. The following year, at the age of seventeen, Susan joined her. Susan and Daniel left Battenville on a snowy day in November, both wearing traditional Quaker clothing: he, a black suit and broad-brimmed hat, she a drab gray dress and bonnet. They set off in an uncovered horse-drawn wagon, with blankets on their laps to keep them warm. In Albany, they boarded a steamboat to take them south. After journeying for several days, they arrived at the school and reunited with Guelma.

Woodcut showing traditional Quaker dress, 1836, artist unknown

A Quaker Girlhood

When it came time to say goodbye to her father, Susan experienced a sudden and painful bout of homesickness. "Oh, what pangs were felt," she wrote in her diary, "it seemed impossible for me to part with him. I could not speak to bid him farewell." Shortly after he left, Daniel wrote to his daughters that he hoped Susan felt better. She didn't. A week later, she still felt as if she were "taking leave of him again." The intensity of her homesickness took her by surprise: She hadn't understood the depth of her attachment to her father until the time came to say goodbye.

2
The Financial Crisis

"I think the girl who is able to earn her own living and pay her own way should be as happy as anybody on earth. The sense of independence and security is very sweet."
—*Susan B. Anthony*

Educating girls in the nineteenth century—those who were not enslaved—generally meant teaching them the arts necessary to be a wife and mother: sewing, spinning, embroidery, cooking, home remedies, and household management. Middle- and upper-class girls were often taught basic reading and writing, particularly in the North, where literacy rates among whites were higher than in the South. In addition, upper-class girls might be taught poetry, literature, history, and politics, but they understood that as

The Financial Crisis

women they were expected to stay out of public life and public discourse.

Deborah Moulson's Female Seminary in Hamilton, Pennsylvania, in contrast, was founded in the spirit of Quaker liberalism. Susan and her classmates studied chemistry, astronomy, history, arithmetic, geography, literature, and writing. They were also taught the Quaker virtues of humility and hard work—lessons Susan readily absorbed. "Five weeks have been spent in Hamilton and to what purpose?" she wrote earnestly to her family. "Has my mind advanced either in virtue or literature? I fear that every moment has not been profitably spent. O, may this careless mind be more watchful in the future!"

About this time, Susan dropped her middle name, Brownell, which she never liked, and replaced it with a B., renaming herself Susan B. Anthony.

One day in 1838, activist Lucretia Mott came to speak to the students at the Female Seminary. Mott lectured the girls on the importance of

Lucretia Mott, Quaker activist and early women's rights advocate, painted by Joseph Kyle, 1842

women improving their intellects. Mott boldly disregarded the contemporary notion that women were supposed to stay out of politics. She had founded the Philadelphia Female Anti-Slavery Society because women were not allowed leadership positions in the American Anti-Slavery Society.

While Susan loved learning, she was unhappy in the school. No matter how much effort she put into her schoolwork, the head teacher, Deborah Moulson, found fault. The constant criticism wore her down. Guelma, in contrast, was easily able to please her teacher. Susan—outspoken as always—confronted Moulson and demanded to know why Guelma earned constant praise while she nothing but criticism. Moulson replied sternly in the formal Quaker manner of speaking: "Thy sister Guelma does the best she is capable of, but thou dost not. Thou has greater abilities and I demand the best of thy capability." If Susan resented being held to a higher standard, she never said so, but she often complained that she couldn't please her teacher. Moulson's constant criticism made Susan painfully aware of her own shortcomings.

★ ★ ★ ★ ★ ★ ★ ★ ★ ★ ★ ★ ★ ★

Meanwhile, the nation was experiencing its first major financial crisis, and as a result, Daniel's factories ran

The Times, by Edward Williams Clay, published by H. R. Robinson, 1837. Illustration showing the financial panic of 1837, with people begging in the streets.

into trouble. The crisis started with President Andrew Jackson's decision to shut down the national bank. Jackson believed that banks were evil and served the interest of what he called the moneyed elite and industrialists. His opinion was that what benefited factory owners and bankers harmed the factory workers and day laborers—and he declared himself a champion of the common man.

When Jackson shut down the national bank, he ordered all federal funds moved to state banks. The state banks, not properly regulated, lent out too much money to people who were unable to pay it back. When borrowers were unable to repay their loans, the banks ran out of funds and shut down, causing customers

23

who had deposited money to lose everything. People all over the nation lost their homes and farms. The result was a downward spiral. With so many people unemployed and penniless, there was no longer demand for manufactured goods. Prices plummeted. Markets dried up.

Daniel went from town to town trying to sell his cloth. Unable to find many buyers, he struggled to meet his expenses and pay his workers. Susan had been at the boarding school just a few months when she learned in a letter from home that her father's businesses and fortunes had fallen so far that her family would have to give up their home before the end of the year. "O can I ever forget that loved residence in Battenville, and no more to call it home seems impossible," she wrote in her diary. Before long, Daniel was unable to cover the cost of tuition for his daughters. Guelma, a year ahead in school, was invited to finish out the term as a teacher, but Susan had to return home.

Despite the circumstances, it was a "happy moment" for Susan when Daniel arrived. She and Guelma ran to the gate to meet him. Her father's face, though, was all agony. That was when Susan understood the extent of the family's misfortune. Seeing how "the great depression" had worn her father down,

The Financial Crisis

she wrote in her diary, "O, that he may have the courage to pass through all the trying scenes of life."

After they returned to Battenville, the bankruptcy court ordered an auction to sell all their personal belongings to pay Daniel's creditors. All their possessions were to be sold: their books, including their family Bible; Daniel's spectacles; clothing, even underclothing. Joshua Read, Susan's maternal uncle, came to the rescue. He journeyed to Battenville and saved from the public auction the wedding presents Lucy had received from their parents, mostly furniture and silverware, by claiming that they belonged to him, not his sister Lucy, on the grounds that he was heir and his parents shouldn't have given their daughter such valuables. Later he returned the items to Lucy. He attended the auction, and bought their clothing and books, which he also returned to them.

To bring in badly needed cash, Susan took a job teaching in a Quaker boarding school about ten miles from Battenville. She was rankled to learn that she earned one-quarter the salary men earned for doing the same work, but there was nothing she could do about it. Because she had to live away from home, she again suffered homesickness, but this time she didn't have the nearness of Guelma to comfort her. "I again left home to mingle with strangers," she wrote despondently, "which seems to be my lot." Her homesickness was made worse because of the "embarrassing condition of our business affairs."

Susan moved back home to help when Daniel established a private Quaker boarding school for boys. The financial crash made it difficult to attract paying students, and the small earnings from the school were not enough to support the family, so Daniel decided to move the family to a village called Hardscrabble, about two miles down the Batten Kill River, where he still owned a gristmill. He rented a house for his family to live in, a large house that had been an inn and tavern before the financial crisis. The Anthonys were able to cover some of their expenses by offering lodging to travelers. Daniel's gristmill was heavily mortgaged, but he was able to turn a small profit.

Not long after moving to Hardscrabble, Daniel was appointed town postmaster, a job with no salary, but which allowed the Anthonys the luxury of sending letters without paying postage. To gain a measure of dignity for the town, Daniel worked with the town leaders to have the name changed from Hardscrabble to Center Falls.

Susan plunged back into the daily routine of keeping house for the family and boarders. "Did a large washing to-day,"

The Financial Crisis

she wrote in her journal. "Spent today at the spinning-wheel . . . Baked twenty-one loaves of bread . . . Wove three yards of carpet yesterday." Despite their financial hardships, Susan and her sisters were happy. The Anthonys retained all their friends from their more prosperous days. Susan and her sisters enjoyed buggy rides, visiting neighbors, parties, and picnics. Lucy, whose youngest child was now past babyhood, was also content. Later she said the years in Center Falls were among her happiest.

The family's dire financial situation, though, meant that the older girls must either find paying work or get married. Guelma accepted an offer of marriage from Aaron McLean, Judge McLean's son, who was now a successful businessman. Guelma's engagement left Susan feeling that she'd lost a friend. Some days she'd come home eager to share a bit of news with Guelma only to find Guelma sitting with Aaron in the dining room, their heads together in whispered conversation.

To help with the family finances, Susan moved to New Rochelle, New York, to accept a teaching position there. Her job was the assistant to the schoolmistress, but much of the responsibility for teaching the children fell to her. Susan immediately established herself as outspoken and opinionated.

SUSAN B. ANTHONY

She spoke up when the Friends' Meeting treated a visiting African American rudely. She let the entire meeting know what she thought of their poor manners. "The people about here are anti-abolitionist and anti everything else that's good," she wrote in a letter home. "The Friends raised quite a fuss about a colored man sitting in the meeting house, and some left on account of it . . . What lack of Christianity is this! There are three colored girls who have been in the habit of attending Friends' meetings where they have lived, but they are not allowed to sit even on the back seat." Horrified, Susan added: "One long-faced elder dusted off a seat in the gallery and told them to sit there."

When President Martin Van Buren, formerly Andrew Jackson's vice president, visited New Rochelle, the town welcomed him with parades, bands playing, and cheers. Susan refused to attend. She blamed Van Buren as much as former president Andrew Jackson for her family's financial ruin. She was horrified that a man might be so elevated above others simply by virtue of having been elected president. "Really," she wrote in a letter home, "one would have thought an angelic being had descended from heaven, to have heard and seen the commotion." In the spirit of the Quaker belief in equality for all,

The Financial Crisis

Susan viewed U.S. presidents as "nothing more than ordinary men and therefore should not be worshipped more than any mortal being."

She didn't think much of Martin Van Buren's political opponents either. Kentucky politician Henry Clay had recently founded a new political party called the Whigs to oppose the Democratic Party of Andrew Jackson and Martin Van Buren. Whigs favored a well-regulated national bank and federally funded improvements such as roads and canals. Susan's objection to the Whigs was their hypocrisy and lack of morals. After commenting that Henry Clay attended a festival in which twenty-three hundred bottles of champagne were consumed, she added that "He had a slave with him to wait on him and hand him water to clear out his throat while he was speaking; and this was while he was preaching liberty and declaring what a fine thing this freedom is!"

✶ ✶ ✶ ✶ ✶ ✶ ✶ ✶ ✶ ✶ ✶ ✶ ✶ ✶ ✶

Susan finished the term and returned home to attend Guelma's wedding, held on September 19, 1839. To strangers, casual acquaintances, colleagues, and her students, Susan now became Miss Anthony instead of Miss Susan.

SUSAN B. ANTHONY

After Guelma's wedding, Anthony accepted a teaching position in the home of an Albany merchant. While teaching and helping to take care of the merchant's children, she continued studying to improve her own intellect. She visited Guelma and Aaron in Battenville, and told them about her new achievement: She had learned to do algebra. Aaron was not impressed. That evening Anthony helped Guelma prepare dinner. Upon tasting Susan's delicious cream biscuits, he said, "I'd rather see a woman make biscuits like these than solve the knottiest problem in algebra."

"There is no reason," Anthony shot back, "why she should not be able to do both."

The Financial Crisis

According to nineteenth-century protocol, younger unmarried daughters were referred to as "Miss," followed by their first names. The oldest unmarried girl was called "Miss," followed by her last name. Servant girls and those enslaved were always referred to simply by their first names. Historians believe the custom of referring to unmarried women as "Miss" originated with the dawn of the Industrial Revolution in the early nineteenth century so that in cities and factories where young women often lived away from their families, women eligible for marriage could be readily distinguished from those who were not. Married women were known as "Mrs.", followed by their husband's last name. Men, whether married nor not, were referred to as "Mr." and always retained their own names. A married woman taking her husband's name reflected that under legal principle of coverture she no longer had a separate legal existence of her own.

3

An Unconventional Young Woman

"In those days, no man wanted to marry a woman who had 'views.' For any woman to allow it to be known that she cherished 'views' was to condemn her to a single estate for the rest of her days; and this I knew, but still I dared the situation and I have taken the consequences."
— *Susan B. Anthony*

In 1845, Lucy's father died, leaving enough money to relieve the Anthonys' financial woes. The entire estate passed to Lucy's brother, Joshua Read. He said he would use Lucy's portion to buy Lucy and Daniel a farm if Daniel would return to his first profession, farming. Lucy and Daniel agreed to Joshua's conditions. They selected a farm near Rochester, New York, not far from the Erie Canal. Joshua kept title to the property in his name to protect Lucy's home in case Daniel went into business again and failed.

An Unconventional Young Woman

At about this time, Hannah accepted a marriage proposal from Eugene Mosher, a merchant from Easton, New York. Anthony resigned her teaching position and came home to preside over Hannah's wedding preparations, and to help her parents settle into their new Rochester farm.

One day, Anthony was in the parlor working on a feathered star quilt for Hannah's new home when a group of Quakers stopped by to visit. One of the visitors, an elderly widower from Vermont, asked her for a glass of water. He followed her out to the well, where he proposed marriage. She turned him down. He begged her to reconsider. To entice her, he described his many

The Anthonys' farmhouse outside Rochester in Center Falls, circa 1850. Photographer unknown.

SUSAN B. ANTHONY

acres, fine home, and sixty cows. She listened politely, and then assured him that she had no wish to marry. Later, after receiving a proposal from another widower, she remarked that widowers generally proposed marriage because they were looking for a housekeeper—or a housekeeper and nanny if the widower had children. Anthony had no desire to take what she viewed as a permanent unpaid position.

After Hannah's wedding, the Anthonys moved to their new farm. The two youngest, Merritt and Mary, were still unmarried and remained with their parents. The Anthonys' new farm was set on thirty-two acres. The family got right to work putting the house and yard into shape. To get through the first year until they could get the farm producing enough to support the family, Daniel took a teaching job in town.

In April, Joshua Read helped his niece—who was then twenty-six years old—obtain the position of headmistress of the female department of the Canajoharie Academy, a well-respected and widely known institution. Joshua Read was a wealthy and influential member of the nearby community and served as a trustee on the academy's board of directors, so when he recommended Anthony, his recommendation carried weight. It was a prestigious position. The headmistress was

An Unconventional Young Woman

responsible for educating about twenty-five young women. For the first time, Anthony would be teaching older students instead of small children. She felt nervous about whether she was adequately prepared, but she was excited about the opportunity. The position paid well enough so that she could support herself with a comfortable lifestyle.

Canajoharie was a charming village nestled along the banks of the Mohawk River, about a hundred and seventy-five miles from Rochester. This time Anthony separated herself from home more easily, even though Canajoharie was far enough away to make visiting difficult. She boarded with her uncle Joshua and his family.

Her duties included teaching reading, writing, spelling, composition, arithmetic, botany, and history. After her first day, she reported to her uncle, "I am most happy to say to you my confidence in my ability to teach the Canajoharie Misses has increased tenfold since this morning." Her confidence came from finding out that she knew a lot more than her students. "The scholars are not so far advanced as I had anticipated," she said, "rather backward if anything."

It was not a Quaker school, and her Read relatives were not Quaker, so Anthony set aside her Quaker plain clothing. With more spending money than she'd ever had before, she bought fashionable clothes. She wore a new gown that was "plaid, white, blue, purple & brown, has two puffs around the skirt cups to the sleeves, with puffs & buttons." She added that "all say the school marm looks beautiful and I heard some of the scholars expressing fear that someone should be smitten and they thus deprived of a teacher."

She struck others as a woman ruled by logic, serenely self-assured, and dignified. With blue eyes that shone with intelligence and handsome features, she had no shortage of men asking to escort her to dances or parties. She received a marriage proposal soon after arriving at the academy, which she promptly turned down. She described the man as a "real soft-headed old bachelor"—and she had no intention of marrying a man who she did not consider her intellectual equal.

The first time she accepted an invitation to a dance, she had some reservations. She was, after all, a Quaker woman. She felt awkward on the dance floor. About a month later, she accepted an invitation to a military ball. When her escort had too much to drink, she was sorry she'd agreed to accompany him and swore that before she accepted another such offer she "must have a total abstinence man to accompany me. I cannot think of going

An Unconventional Young Woman

to a dance with one whose highest delight is to make a fool of himself."

Her self-confidence grew as she mastered her job and became accustomed to her independence. On her twenty-seventh birthday, she said, "I can see in the mirror I grow older but in feelings I know no change unless it be greater flow of spirits."

✴ ✴ ✴ ✴ ✴ ✴ ✴ ✴ ✴ ✴ ✴ ✴ ✴ ✴ ✴

In April of 1848, New York passed a law allowing married women—under limited circumstances—to own property. If a woman owned property before she was married, she could continue to own it. If she inherited money or property during the marriage, her inheritance was hers. After the law passed, Joshua Read transferred title to the Rochester farm to Lucy as her inheritance from her parents.

In July of that same year, a group of women's rights pioneers held their first meeting in Seneca Falls, New York, less than sixty miles from the Anthonys' farm in Rochester. The meeting was called the Seneca Falls Convention. Anthony learned that one of the organizers was Lucretia Mott, who she'd heard speak at the Female Academy. Anthony didn't attend, but learned from newspaper accounts that the two hundred

SUSAN B. ANTHONY

> The Declaration of Sentiments argued that women's rights flowed from the ideals of equality and self-government upon which America had been founded. The Declaration followed the lead of British writer Mary Wollstonecraft's pamphlet, *A Vindication of the Rights of Woman*, published in 1790, in which she argued that God had given "natural rights" to both men and women, and just as men had the right not to be enslaved by tyrants, women had the right not to be enslaved by men. Wollstonecraft noted that women were treated by society like children instead of adults.
>
> Anthony was one of Wollstonecraft's admirers. Her personal copy of *A Vindication of the Rights of Woman* is housed today in the Susan B. Anthony collection of the Library of Congress.

attendees adopted a Declaration of Sentiments, modeled on the Declaration of Independence, but inserting women: "We hold these truths to be self-evident; that all men and women are created equal . . ." The group proposed that women should be given the rights of citizenship, including the right to vote. Among the speakers on the second day was Frederick Douglass,

An Unconventional Young Woman

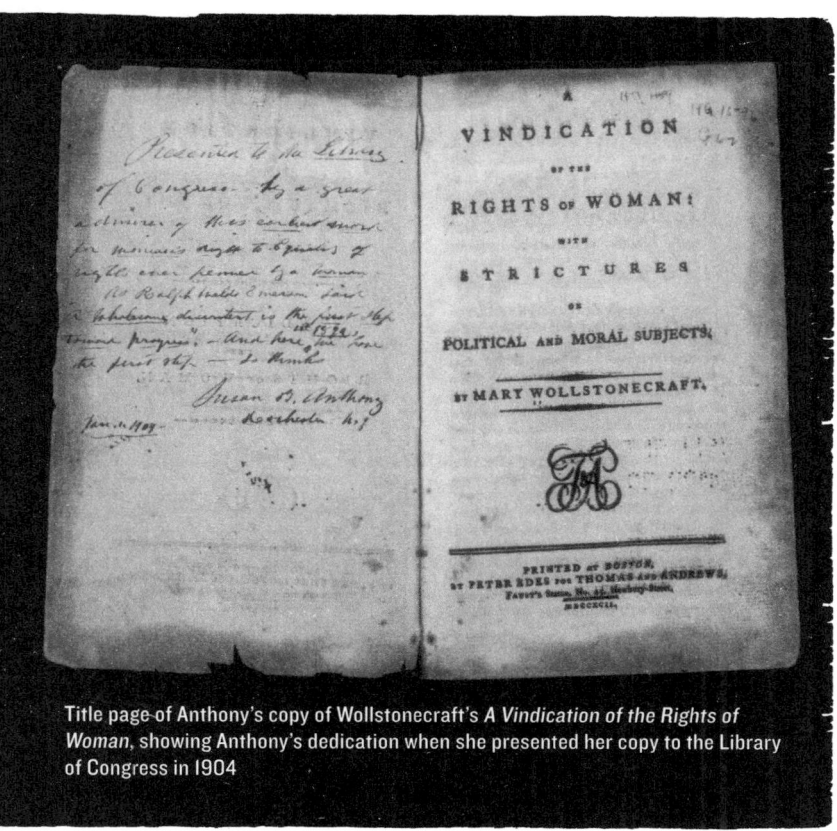

Title page of Anthony's copy of Wollstonecraft's *A Vindication of the Rights of Woman*, showing Anthony's dedication when she presented her copy to the Library of Congress in 1904.

a former slave and now an abolition leader known for his brilliant and fiery speeches. Two weeks later, the convention moved to Rochester, New York. Anthony learned from letters from her family that Daniel, Lucy, and their youngest daughter, Mary, attended the convention and signed the Declaration of Sentiments.

SUSAN B. ANTHONY

Anthony's interest in the condition of women led her to became active in the temperance movement—the movement to outlaw alcohol. She had seen firsthand what happened when men drank too much (and in the nineteenth century, most alcoholics were men). Unable to hold a job, alcoholics sank into poverty, which in turn left their wives and children in poverty. Many alcoholics also became abusive and battered their wives, who were unable to leave their marriages because of the difficulty of obtaining a divorce. Many wives of drunks reported that they took jobs to support the family, only to have their husbands take their money to buy alcohol. Anthony's solution was to outlaw alcohol and preach the need to abstain from drinking it.

Anthony delivered her first public address on March 2, 1849, to a group of women assembled for a temperance meeting. She spoke passionately about "the day when our brothers and sons shall no longer be allured from the right by corrupting influence" of alcohol so that "our sisters and daughters shall no longer be exposed to the half-inebriated seducer." After that, she spoke regularly at temperance meetings and banquets.

Teaching and running the school, though, took most of her

An Unconventional Young Woman

time, limiting what she was able to do on behalf of temperance. As a result, she was growing restless in her job. "I am tired of theory," she wrote to her parents. "I want to hear how we must act to have a happier and more glorious world . . . reform, reform needs to be the watch word."

During her third year teaching at the academy, Anthony's cousin Margaret, Joshua Read's daughter, had a difficult pregnancy. Margaret, who already had three children, lived just across the river, in Palatine Bridge. Anthony nursed Margaret through her illness. One day, Margaret's husband, Joseph, remarked that he had a headache. Margaret replied that she'd had a headache for a week. "Oh," Joseph said, "mine is the real headache, genuine pain, yours is sort of a natural consequence."

Anthony was with Margaret all through the birth. When Margaret failed to recover her strength after giving birth to a daughter, Anthony took over her household duties. While continuing with her teaching, Anthony did all the washing, cleaning, and cooking for Margaret's family. Joseph took for granted that Anthony would willingly and gladly do his housekeeping without thanks or praise. He thought of her as an "old maid," the term applied to older women who never married, and he assumed that an old maid would feel grateful for the opportunity to step into a housewife's duties. "It seems to me," Anthony wrote to her brother Daniel, "that no one feels that it is anything out of the common course of things for me to sacrifice my every feeling, almost every principle, to gratify those with whom I mingle." To her mother, she remarked that there were "drawbacks to marriage which make a woman quite content to remain single."

Margaret died seven weeks after the baby's birth. Anthony grieved deeply. She stayed with Margaret's family through the

> According to some estimates, as many as one out of a hundred women in the nineteenth century died in childbirth. Women are susceptible to infection during childbirth and immediately after. Before the invention of penicillin, infections were often deadly. Puerperal or childbed fever was much feared in the early nineteenth century. Only women attended births. Midwives—women experienced with childbirth—took charge of the delivery. The entire subject of childbearing was considered unpleasant, unfit for polite society, and generally avoided by men.

An Unconventional Young Woman

funeral and until all the children, including the newborn, had been parceled out to relatives. After his children were placed with relatives, Joseph made plans to head west in search of gold, which had recently been discovered in California.

✱ ✱ ✱ ✱ ✱ ✱ ✱ ✱ ✱ ✱ ✱ ✱ ✱ ✱ ✱

Later, when asked why she never married, Anthony gave various explanations. One of her answers was "I'm sure no man could have made me any happier than I have been." She often commented that she'd never met a man who was looking for a companion he would consider an equal. Other times she speculated that her outspoken nature and Quaker views made her unappealing. "Being a Quakeress set me apart, and I think that no one even thought that I, with my tongue, would make a good mistress for a [house]." She observed that her outspoken nature signaled that she would not "slip easily into submission and dependence."

After she became politically active, her answer to the question of why she never married became tinged with politics. "I would not consent that the man I loved," she said, "described in the Constitution as a white male, native born, American citizen, possessed of the right of self government, eligible to the office of the president of the Great Republic, should unite his destinies in marriage with a political slave and pariah. No, no; when I am crowned with all the rights, privileges, and immunities of a citizen, I may give some consideration . . . but until then I must concentrate all my energies on the enfranchisement of my own sex."

4
All the Good You Can

"It is only through a wholesome discontent with things as they are, that we ever try to make them any better."
—*Susan B. Anthony*

Anthony was growing tired of teaching, so her parents offered her an arrangement: If she would come home and run the farm for a year, at the end of the year, she could live at home and pursue her own interests. Daniel had found a business opportunity in Syracuse working for the New York Life Insurance Company, and he wanted some time to build this career. All the Anthony children were married or working away from home. Lucy's health was growing frail, so she couldn't run the farm without help.

SUSAN B. ANTHONY

Anthony took her parents up on the offer. At the end of the teaching term, she resigned from the Canajoharie Academy. The school held a farewell banquet for her. She was surprised and flattered when a speaker at the banquet declared that "Miss Anthony is the smartest woman who ever has been in Canajoharie."

She returned to Rochester and threw herself into farmwork. She ran the farm the way she had managed the school—with enormous competence and focus. She was delighted to find that the peach saplings the family had planted when they'd first moved to Rochester had grown into an abundant orchard. She put aside her fashionable clothing, donned a plain calico dress, and spent much of September picking, preserving, and canning peaches.

Frederick Douglass, photographed by John White Hurn, 1862

Shortly after she arrived in Rochester, her father took her to the home of Frederick Douglass to meet the famous abolitionist. In 1847, Douglass had settled in Rochester and founded his newspaper, the *North Star*. Partly because of Douglass, Rochester had become known as

All the Good You Can

a hotbed of abolitionism. The *New York Herald* denounced the radicals of Rochester, advising the town to throw its "N— printing press" into Lake Ontario, and banish Frederick Douglass to Canada.

Along with the *North Star*, the Anthonys were also devoted readers of William Lloyd Garrison's newspaper, the *Liberator*. Garrison, like Douglass, was considered one of the nation's most radical abolitionists. Others who were antislavery put forward proposals such as gradual emancipation, where slaves are freed under laws that, for example, would give each slave his or her freedom at the age of twenty-eight, thus gradually phasing out slavery. Some who wanted to end slavery proposed that slave owners be compensated for the loss of their "property." Garrison rejected the very idea that human beings could be property, and thus he denounced any emancipation plans that included compensating slave owners for their losses. He called for the immediate end of slavery.

The Anthony farmhouse was a popular meeting place for the local abolitionists, who gathered there for Sunday dinners. Douglass was a frequent guest. When Garrison visited Rochester, he too came for dinner. Among their guests were also Amy and Isaac Post, who often gave shelter to runaway slaves. Some of the guests at the Anthonys' dinners knew the location of a station along the Underground Railroad—highly secret information known only to a handful of the most trusted abolitionists.

At the end of Anthony's first year at home, her father resumed management of the farm. While continuing to help out at home, she became active in the local Daughters of Temperance movement, and in 1849 she was elected president of the Rochester branch. She organized temperance societies in thirty counties, appointing sixty women, two from each county, to serve as canvassing captains. She was thus able to obtain thousands of signatures within weeks, an impressive feat in an era before telephones. For a petition demanding the complete prohibition of alcohol, she obtained more than twenty-eight thousand signatures, which she presented to lawmakers.

She also attended antislavery meetings. In 1851, she went on a weeklong tour with a group of Quaker abolitionists to speak at meetinghouses throughout the region. Her life became a tireless round of organizing and attending meetings, gathering signatures on petitions, and delivering speeches.

Photographs of her from this period show her as severe and serious. She tended to hold back during a discussion, wait for the right moment, and then deliver a pithy and penetrating comment. Her contemporaries described her as aloof, reserved, stately, brilliant, and "the perfection of common sense." Her critics called her a "strong-minded woman," which was intended to be a slur against her femininity and not a compliment. She was described by one newspaper as having "pleasing rather than pretty features" and a "decidedly expressive countenance." She preferred to be photographed in profile because her right eye still tended to wander.

Anthony thought of herself as a "reformer," by which she meant someone who works to improve society. Throughout the country, though, particularly the South, Anthony and those who shared her views were seen as dangerous radicals intent on overthrowing deeply rooted American traditions.

Occasionally Anthony took a short-term teaching job, but because her parents supported her work and she used the farm as her home base, she didn't have to worry about money. Her father often brought home bolts of dress material, so she always had enough clothing to wear. She covered her expenses by charging a small admission to her lectures. More than once, as Anthony was leaving the farm to set out on a tour or to attend a convention, her mother said to her, "Go do all the good you can."

★ ★ ★ ★ ★ ★ SUSAN B. ANTHONY ★ ★ ★ ★ ★ ★

★ ★ ★ ★ ★ ★ ★ ★ ★ ★ ★ ★ ★ ★ ★ ★

In her travels, Anthony befriended Amelia Bloomer, an ardent abolitionist who was famous for a new article of clothing. Nineteenth-century women wore long, heavy skirts that restricted movement and limited the activities they could perform. Many women also wore corsets intended to force the body into an hourglass shape. Corsets, which were extremely uncomfortable, made breathing difficult, with the result that women

---

Anthony considered herself a reformer—another word for liberal. The political spectrum is generally pictured as a straight line, with moderates in the middle, liberals to the left, and conservatives to the right.

POLITICAL LEFT   **CENTER**   **POLITICAL RIGHT**

RADICAL — LIBERAL — MODERATE — CONSERVATIVE — REACTIONARY

On the political left side of the spectrum, liberals are comfortable with change, and look for changes that they

who wore them often lost consciousness and fainted if they were startled or shocked. The frequent fainting of women contributed to the widespread belief that they were frail and delicate. Girls as young as seven were laced into overly tight corsets. Because of the general shame and secrecy surrounding pregnancy, maternity corsets were designed to minimize the pregnancy and keep the female body in its pre-pregnancy shape as long as possible. Later it was discovered that the corsets—laced too tightly—caused

believe will improve society. Radicals want to bring about swift changes, looking eagerly ahead to what they believe will be a better world. On the political right, conservatives are less comfortable with change. Reactionaries long nostalgically for the past—a time they believe things used to be better. They want to retreat to the past and restore the order of how things used to be. Those in the middle, moderates, shy away from extreme views.

Liberals and radicals welcome change partly because they tend to see history as evolving and improving. Conservatives, in contrast, want to maintain the status quo, and reactionaries want to retreat to the past.

internal damage to a woman's organs, and that maternity corsets harmed growing fetuses.

Amelia Bloomer, tired of uncomfortable and restrictive clothing, copied a style of dress first sported by a New Yorker named Elizabeth Smith Miller: a knee-length dress with the lower leg covered by baggy pants. Amelia Bloomer insisted she should not get the credit for the outfit because she didn't invent it. But she published her own newspaper and touted the benefits of being released from restrictive clothing, so she was the one who made the outfit famous. The outfit thus came to be

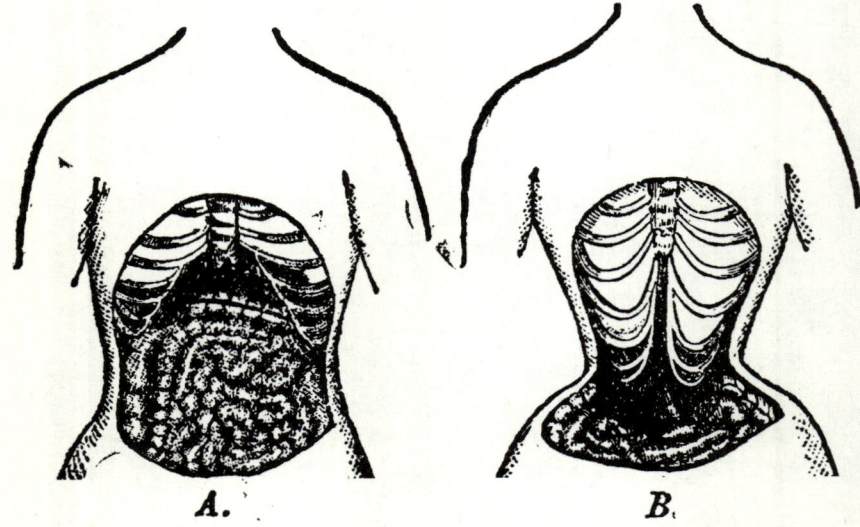

"Nature Versus Corsets, Illustrated," showing the effect of a corset on the internal organs, published in a Library of Congress "Guide for the Study of Women and Culture in the United States," 2001

Advertisement for a corset, created about 1887

SUSAN B. ANTHONY

called bloomers. America witnessed a "bloomer craze" associated with radical women bent on defying cultural norms. Women wearing bloomers were the target of jokes and satiric cartoons. In the streets, men stared, jibed, ridiculed, and even attacked women who wore bloomers. Cartoonists portrayed bloomer-wearing women as doing the devil's work of inducing women to act like men.

Anthony became a fan of bloomers. Wearing them infused her with a new sense of freedom. Bloomer wearers next began cutting their hair into short, easy-to-care-for bobs. Anthony cut her hair as well.

Anthony, wearing her bloomers, took to touring upstate New York during the long, brutal winters. She had to brave freezing weather and snowstorms, but in winter, the inhabitants of isolated villages were eager for any diversion at all. Being cooped up inside

Woodcut portrait of Amelia Bloomer wearing bloomers, published in the *Lily*, September 9, 1851

combined with the novelty of a female political speaker was often enough to prompt local residents to bundle up and wade through the snow to hear her speak.

Upon arriving in a village, Anthony checked to see that the notices she'd sent ahead were posted. Then she made sure the local church or hall she'd rented was in order, and put the finishing touches on her speech. Sometimes when Anthony arrived in a new place, she was met with enthusiasm, as when a group of women wearing bloomers came to greet her. Other times she was met with hostility, as when a preacher angrily told her that "If the Bible teaches anything it is that women should be quiet keepers at home and not go gadding around the country."

In May of 1851, Anthony and Amelia Bloomer visited Seneca Falls to attend a meeting organized by William Lloyd Garrison. After the meeting, while standing on a street corner, they saw Elizabeth Cady Stanton, one of the leaders in the women's rights movement, and the author of the 1848 Declaration of Rights and Sentiments. Years later, Stanton described when she first met Anthony:

> *How well I remember the day! George Thompson and William Lloyd Garrison having announced an anti-slavery*

meeting in Seneca Falls, Miss Anthony came to attend it. These gentlemen were my guests. Walking home after the adjournment, we met Mrs. Bloomer and Miss Anthony, on the corner of the street, waiting to greet us.

There she stood, with her good earnest face and genial smile, dressed in gray delaine, hat and all the same color, relieved with pale blue ribbons, the perfection of neatness and sobriety. I liked her thoroughly, and why I did not at once invite her home with me to dinner I do not know . . .

During that first uneventful meeting, Anthony had no premonition that she and Elizabeth Cady Stanton would soon enter a friendship that would last more than fifty years, and that together they would lead the charge of a women's revolution.

5
A Nation in Need of Reform

"Our mission is to deepen sympathy and convert it into right action, to show that the men and women of the North are slave-holders, those of the South slave-owners. The guilt rests on the North equally with the South, therefore our work is to rouse the sleeping conscience of the North."

—*Susan B. Anthony*

The same year Anthony met Stanton, 1851, Sojourner Truth caught the attention of the nation's reformers when she and a group of women tried to hold a political meeting in a church in Akron, Ohio. Truth had been born into slavery in about 1797 under the name Isabella Baumfree. At the age of nine, she was sold at an auction along with a flock of sheep. In 1826, she escaped to freedom with her infant daughter. She changed her name to Sojourner Truth, and became a fighter for abolition and women's rights.

★ ★ ★ ★ ★ ★ SUSAN B. ANTHONY ★ ★ ★ ★ ★ ★

Sojourner Truth, photo created in 1864, photographer unknown

The women trying to hold their meeting in Akron were unable to concentrate because of the jeering and heckling of a band of men. The hecklers insisted that women were too delicate for politics, and moreover, should be in their proper places in the home. All eyes were on Sojourner Truth when she pointed her finger at the hecklers and said,

That man over there says that women need to be helped into carriages, and lifted over ditches, and to have the best place everywhere. Nobody ever helps me into carriages, or over mud-puddles, or gives me any best place! And arn't I a woman? Look at me! Look at my arm! I have ploughed and planted, and gathered into barns, and no man [can better] me! And arn't I a woman? I could work as much and eat as much as a man—when I could get it—and bear the lash as well! And arn't I a woman? I have borne thirteen children, and seen most all sold off to slavery, and

A Nation in Need of Reform

when I cried out with my mother's grief, none but Jesus heard me! And arn't I a woman?

Sojourner Truth "was black and she was a woman," Anthony and her colleagues wrote later in the *History of Woman Suffrage*, "and all the insults that could be cast upon color and sex were together hurled at her, but there she stood, calm and dignified."

Newspapers widely ridiculed women who ventured from the private sphere. Anthony attended the 1852 National Women's Rights Convention, which the *Syracuse Star* called the "Tomfoolery Convention" and described the attendees as "poor creatures who take part in the silly rant of brawling women." Men who attended the convention were "Aunt Nancy men . . . of such damnable doctrines and accursed heresies as would make demons of the pit shudder to hear." The *New York Herald* called the convention a "farce" and explained what was wrong with both abolitionists and women's rights reformers:

How did woman first become subject to man, as she now is all over the world? By her nature, her sex, just as the negro is and always will be to the end of time, inferior to the white race and, therefore, doomed to subjection.

SUSAN B. ANTHONY

The abolitionists and the women's rights reformers were up against two deeply held cultural norms: paternalism and the idea of separate spheres.

Paternalism held that there was a natural hierarchy in society with white men at the top and black women at the bottom. Under the doctrine of paternalism, blacks, women, and Native Americans were inferior to white men and needed their care and protection. Paternalism was based on the belief that white women and all people of color were better off (and happier) under the dominion of white men.

★ ★ ★ ★ ★ ★ ★ ★ ★ ★ ★ ★ ★ ★ ★

Anthony met Elizabeth Cady Stanton again when she and Amelia Bloomer visited Seneca Falls. Stanton invited a small group of women to her house—Anthony, Bloomer, and a few others. Anthony listened as a charming and gregarious Stanton talked about how deeply moved she'd been as a child when she'd listened to the pitiful stories of women who came to her father's law office begging for help. Many of the women had inherited money, which their husbands were squandering. Stanton's father

A Nation in Need of Reform

> Male-female roles were described as separate spheres, an idea that had deep roots in American and European society and gained strength during the Industrial Revolution of the early nineteenth century. Women were said to inhabit the private sphere of home and church. Men inhabited the public sphere of industry, commerce, and politics. Part of the rationale for separate spheres was that women were thought to be more fragile and virtuous than men, so they must be placed on a pedestal and protected from the often ugly world of politics and business. As Sojourner Truth pointed out, the so-called pedestal was for white women only.

told the women that under the law as it stood, there was nothing he could do to help them.

Stanton, who had been born into an upper-class family, was a gracious hostess and personally knew the most important

Elizabeth Cady Stanton with her daughter Harriot Stanton Blatch, 1856

SUSAN B. ANTHONY

people in the state. She had received a top-notch education and graduated from Emma Willard's Troy Female Seminary, and was immediately drawn to politics. She learned the art of lawyerly arguments from her father, and became expert at arguing in the alternative—throwing out lots of arguments to see which would stick. When she married abolitionist Henry Stanton, she insisted on leaving "obey" out of her marriage vows. Her husband, though, was not supportive of her women's rights activism. Her father, downright hostile, threatened to disinherit her if she continued rabbling for women's rights.

Stanton was widely known for hosting gatherings at her home. William Lloyd Garrison's son later compared her to a famous Frenchwoman, Madame de Staël, a brilliant member of the aristocracy who was highly critical of the ruling government, and became famous for her "salons" in which artists, writers, and others gathered to discuss the pressing issues of the day.

Not long after Anthony visited Stanton's home in Seneca Falls, Stanton wrote to Anthony—who was on the road lecturing—"I will gladly do all in my power to aid you. Work down this way, then you come & stay with me . . . I will assist you in getting up such a lecture as you desire."

Susan B. Anthony at the age of thirty-six, photographer unknown

★ ★ ★ ★ ★ ★ **SUSAN B. ANTHONY** ★ ★ ★ ★ ★ ★

So began a friendship in which their personalities complemented and balanced each other.

While Stanton was most comfortable at home and at her writing desk, Anthony preferred action—speaking, canvassing, and agitating. Stanton gave Anthony credit for keeping her in the public arena. Stanton, the mother of seven children, wrote in her memoirs, "With the cares of a large family, I might, in time, like too many women, have become wholly absorbed in a narrow family selfishness" without Anthony prodding her along.

Anthony often stayed with Stanton at her home in Seneca Falls. After Stanton's children were in bed, Stanton and Anthony worked far into the night. During the days, Anthony sometimes took care of Stanton's children so that Stanton could have a turn at the desk. In her *Reminiscences*, Stanton wrote, "It was mid such exhilarating scenes that Miss Anthony and I wrote addresses for temperance, anti-slavery, educational and woman's rights conventions. Here we forged resolutions, protests, appeals, petitions, agricultural reports and constitutional arguments." Any time Stanton looked out the window and saw "that stately Quaker girl" coming across her lawn, she'd feel a surge of excitement.

★ ★ ★ ★ ★ ★ ★ ★ ★ ★ ★ ★ ★ ★ ★ ★

A Nation in Need of Reform

Anthony attended the two-day New York State Teachers' Convention in Rochester beginning August 3, 1853. She paid the price of admission and took her seat. There were five hundred teachers in Corinthian Hall, two-thirds of them women. The men sat in front and did all the speaking. The women sat in the back, listening. "My heart was filled with grief and indignation," Anthony wrote, "thus to see the minority, simply because they were men, presuming that in them was vested all the wisdom and knowledge . . . And what was most humiliating was to look into the faces of these women and see that by far the larger proportion were perfectly satisfied with the position assigned to them."

Presiding over the meeting was a math teacher, Charles Davies, a graduate of West Point, wearing full military dress. Anthony listened to the men discussing why teachers had so little respect compared to doctors and lawyers, and debating how to remedy the situation.

Then she stood up, and in a calm and clear voice, said, "Mr. President."

The assembly, shocked to hear a woman's voice, fell silent. Davies, thrown into confusion, asked, "What will the lady have?"

SUSAN B. ANTHONY

"I wish, sir," she said, "to speak to the question under discussion."

For a half hour, the men debated whether to allow her to speak. Anthony sat down and waited for the verdict. At last, the men decided she should be permitted to offer her views. So she stood back up, and said,

> It seems to me, gentlemen, that none of you quite comprehend the cause of the disrespect of which you complain. Do you not see that so long as society says a woman is incompetent to be a lawyer, minister, or doctor, but has ample ability to be a teacher, that every man of you who chooses this profession tacitly acknowledges that he has no more brains than a woman?
>
> And this, too, is the reason that teaching is a less lucrative profession, as here men must compete with the cheap labor of woman. Would you exalt your profession, exalt those who labor with you. Would you make it more lucrative, increase the salaries of the women engaged in the noble work of educating our future Presidents, Senators, and Congressmen.

A Nation in Need of Reform

This bombshell was followed by the "profoundest silence." Then three men stood up and rushed to congratulate her—and to tell her she was right. The majority of those present, though, including many of the women, were not pleased. "I felt so mortified," one of the women said later, "I really wished the floor would open and swallow me up." Another worried that the compliments would encourage Anthony to continue such undignified behavior.

By the next morning, Charles Davies had recovered from his shock, and had his response ready. He stood at the front of the hall wearing his resplendent military uniform. After opening the proceedings, he said, "I have been asked why no provisions have been made for female lecturers before this association and why ladies are not appointed on the committees." He paused for dramatic effect, and concluded with "I would not think of dragging women from their pedestals into the dust."

✯ ✯ ✯ ✯ ✯ ✯ ✯ ✯ ✯ ✯ ✯ ✯ ✯ ✯ ✯

Reluctantly Anthony gave up wearing bloomers. "The attention of my audience was fixed upon my clothes," she said, "instead of my words." She returned to Quaker-style

★★★★★ SUSAN B. ANTHONY ★★★★★

clothing, which, for her, represented simplicity, earnestness, hard work, and dedication.

To talk to women about their natural rights as human beings, she went from house to house, knocking on the doors of cottages, farmhouses, and mansions. She traveled in stagecoaches, open wagons, and sleighs. As she traveled from town to town and spent time in countless kitchens talking to one woman after another, she came to recognize the importance of a woman having money of her own. She concluded that it was a woman's poverty that made her vulnerable, with women from the impoverished classes most susceptible to being abused and exploited by men.

Often Anthony would knock on a door only to have a woman angrily insist that she had all the rights she wanted, and then slam the door in Anthony's face. Anthony understood that the women's movement faced a unique challenge: A sizable percentage of women agreed that women belonged in the domestic sphere. A woman named Sarah Hale published an influential magazine called *Godey's Lady's Book*, telling women that a "true woman" was "delicate and timid." She "required protection" and "possessed a sweet dependency." A true woman, according to Hale, "had charming and insinuating manners." Wives (those

A Nation in Need of Reform

who were white and middle- to upper-class) were seen as morally superior to their husbands—gentler, kinder, more nurturing, the moral compass within the home.

Anthony believed, in the future, a "new true woman" would arise, a woman who would "be her own individual self,—do her own individual work, stand or fall by her own individual wisdom and strength." No longer completely dependent upon man and subservient to him, the new true woman would "use, worthily, every talent given to her by God, in the great work of life, to the best advantage of herself and the race." The new true woman would be able to marry and still enjoy all the same rights her husband enjoyed. Or she could enter any profession, sign contracts, avail herself of the courts, and live independently.

In striving to make women aware of the plight of their condition, Anthony knew she had "embarked in an unpopular cause and must be content to row upstream." She found the courage and energy to plod on by telling herself that she was working, not for her contemporaries, who might never understand or appreciate the work, but—as she explained once in a speech—"for future generations must we labor."

Spending months at a time on the road, and having doors closed in her face was disheartening at times. "I have *very weak* moments," she wrote to Stanton, "and long to lay my weary head somewhere and nestle my full soul close to that of another in full sympathy—I sometimes fear that, I too, shall faint by the wayside—and drop out of the ranks of the faithful few. There is so much, mid all that is hopeful, to discourage & dishearten—and I feel *alone*."

★ ★ ★ ★ ★ ★ ★ ★ ★ ★ ★ ★ ★ ★ ★ ★

In 1856, Anthony became an agent for the American Anti-Slavery Society. She drew a small salary and toured to speak about the evils of slavery.

She saw the workings of slavery for herself when she traveled to Washington, D.C., and Baltimore with friend and fellow reformer Ernestine Rose. They wanted to see if they would find receptive audiences in Washington, D.C., and Maryland for their antislavery and women's rights message. The answer, they soon learned, was no. They were warned in threatening terms by local residents not to speak against slavery, particularly in Maryland. They tried to arrange women's rights meetings, but churches and lecture halls would not allow them to rent space. When they did secure space, newspapers obligingly put notices in the papers, but nobody came to hear them.

A Nation in Need of Reform

Anthony had been assured by proslavery advocates in the North that if she visited a slave state and saw for herself how well the institution worked, she'd have a different opinion of human bondage. One day, to test this theory for herself, she questioned a hotel chambermaid, Sarah, who was cleaning Anthony's room while a little boy played nearby. Sarah told Anthony that she and the boy, who was not her son, were both enslaved. The hotel proprietor rented her from her owner for eight dollars per month. The only money she got for her own pockets was whatever her white masters chose to give her. The boy and his mother, who worked as a cook, belonged to the proprietor. The boy's father, though, belonged to someone on the eastern shore who never allowed him to visit his wife and child.

Anthony felt her "blood chilled" as she listened. "How strangely blind must the person be," she wrote that evening in her journal, "who hates slavery less, by coming in closer contact with its degrading influence." After seeing how easily people could become accustomed to being served by those in bondage, she wrote in her diary, "Oh, Slavery, hateful thing that thou art thus to blunt the keen edge of conscience."

✯ ✯ ✯ ✯ ✯ ✯ ✯ ✯ ✯ ✯ ✯ ✯ ✯ ✯ ✯

★ ★ ★ ★ ★ ★ SUSAN B. ANTHONY ★ ★ ★ ★ ★ ★

As she traveled through New England, Anthony gathered signatures for a personal liberty bill to protect slaves who ran away to the North. She preached a message of empathy and humanity: "We ask you to feel as if you, yourselves, were the slaves," she told her audiences. "The politician talks of slavery as he does of United States banks, tariff, or any other commercial question. We demand the abolition of slavery because the slave is a human being and because man should not hold property in his fellowman."

It was commonly argued that freeing the slaves and allowing them to remain in the United States would create more problems than it would solve. According to this argument, free blacks living alongside whites would create "race-based politics" and would ultimately degrade the white race. Indeed, the very idea of freeing the slaves and giving them political freedom, including the right to vote, struck terror into the hearts of white southerners, particularly in those areas of the South where blacks outnumbered whites. Northerners were afraid that hordes of freed slaves would pour into their states, looking for work, bringing poverty and crime.

Anthony attacked the question of what was to be done with the freed slaves with her usual straightforwardness. "What is

A Nation in Need of Reform

to be done with the freed slaves?" she asked her audiences. "Do with them precisely what you would do with the Irish, the Scotch, and the Germans—Educate them. Welcome them to all the blessings of our free institutions—to our schools & churches, to every department of industry, trade and art." She added, moreover, that "What arrogance in us to put the question, what shall we do with a race of men and women who have fed, clothed and supported both themselves and their oppressors for centuries."

The question of what was to be done with the blacks, Anthony thus insisted, was up to the blacks—and believing otherwise was to continue the paternalistic myth that it was appropriate for some people, because they were inherently superior, to control the fates of others.

✯ ✯ ✯ ✯ ✯ ✯ ✯ ✯ ✯ ✯ ✯ ✯ ✯ ✯ ✯

By the end of 1857, Anthony found herself in financial trouble. She was not earning enough from the price of admission to her talks or her small salary from the Anti-Slavery Society to cover the cost of her travels. She thus found herself with a large deficit. Learning of this, the American Anti-Slavery Society sent her the money she needed with a letter saying, "We

★ ★ ★ ★ ★ ★ SUSAN B. ANTHONY ★ ★ ★ ★ ★ ★

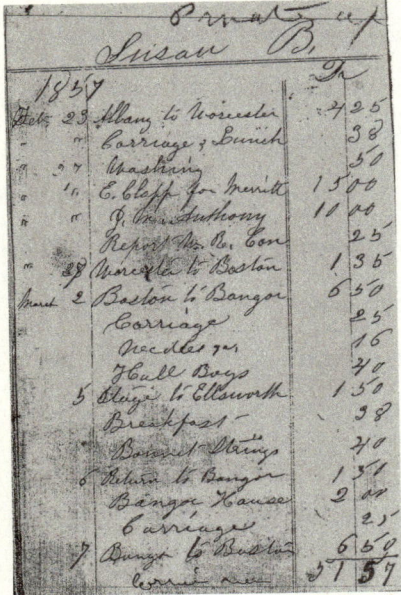

Anthony kept meticulous records all of her life, detailing all of her expenses down to the penny. This is an example of one of her ledger sheets.

cheerfully pay your expenses and want to keep you at the head of the work."

The following year, the leaders of the women's rights movement were surprised and delighted to receive their first large donation—thousands of dollars from a wealthy donor who urged them to use the money "wisely and efficiently" in the interest of women's equality. The donor, Francis Jackson, learned firsthand about the inequality in marriage and child custody laws when his son-in-law mistreated his daughter, and then, taking advantage of the laws in Massachusetts, removed his children from their mother and refused to let the mother or her family see them. Jackson experienced the pain of losing his grandchildren, and he saw his daughter's grief and despair at being separated from her children. Jackson donated the money when he learned that Anthony, Stanton, and

A Nation in Need of Reform

others were working to change the unequal divorce and child custody laws.

✹ ✹ ✹ ✹ ✹ ✹ ✹ ✹ ✹ ✹ ✹ ✹ ✹ ✹ ✹

Once again, in 1858, Anthony attended the New York State Teachers' Convention. Prior to the convention, she met Stanton in Seneca Falls, and together they wrote a series of resolutions for Anthony to introduce at the conference.

When Anthony took her seat in the convention lecture hall, she was prepared to drop another bombshell. As before, Charles Davies presided, wearing his military uniform. Anthony waited patiently for the right moment, then seized the floor and asked permission to propose new resolutions. Once she was given permission, she began reading her resolutions:

That the exclusion of colored youth from our public schools, academies, colleges and universities is the result of a wicked prejudice.

That the expulsion of Miss Latimer from the normal school at Albany, when after six months of successful scholarship it was discovered that colored blood coursed in her veins, was mean and cruel.

Before she finished, there was an uproar in the room. The very idea of fully integrating the state schools and giving black students and black teachers equal status to the whites, stunned and alarmed the audience.

Once again, Anthony had managed to fluster Charles Davies. Finding his voice, he retorted that what she proposed would be a "vast social evil." He had no choice, though, but to refer her resolutions to a committee, where they were defeated.

Stanton, from her home in Seneca Falls, was delighted to read an account of what had happened. "I did indeed see by the papers," Stanton wrote to Anthony, "that you had once more stirred that pool of intellectual stagnation, the educational convention."

6
Civil War

"Organize, agitate, educate must be our war cry."
—*Susan B. Anthony*

It was 1860, the year of a presidential election. Because the proslavery voters could not settle on a single candidate, there were three proslavery candidates. Of the four serious contenders for the presidency, only Republican candidate Abraham Lincoln declared himself opposed to slavery, and even he was tepid about it. While Lincoln was adamant about keeping slavery out of the North and out of the territories, he declared that he had no intention to disturb slavery where it already existed. His reason was that the Constitution as handed down by the Founding Fathers allowed for slavery, so he was obliged to honor it.

> In the nineteenth century, the Democratic Party was the more conservative party, drawing its strength from the South, and from those who sympathized with the Confederate states, and from rural America. The proslavery Democratic Party stood for states' rights on the theory that the federal government had no business interfering with local practices like slavery. The Republican Party, in contrast, represented the interests of the business and banking communities. The Republican Party favored a strong federal government able to make such improvements as roads, railroads, and canals. The Republican Party drew its strength from minority communities, liberal activists, and business communities. The Republican coalition came about because, at the time of the Civil War, minority communities, liberal activists, heavy industry, and banks all shared a need for a strong federal government.

Civil War

With the antislavery vote divided among three candidates, Lincoln won the presidency with less than 40 percent of the popular vote. Within days, the nation was plunged into a crisis. Four days after the election, South Carolina called for a statewide convention to consider seceding from the United States. On December 20, 1860, South Carolina declared itself no longer part of the United States. Within the month, Mississippi, Florida, Alabama, Georgia, Louisiana, and Texas followed. Eventually they would be joined by North Carolina, Arkansas, Virginia, and Tennessee, forming the Confederate States of America.

On a cold evening in Albany in late December, Anthony was out with another reformer, Lydia Mott—cousin of Lucretia Mott—when a heavily veiled woman approached and asked for a private word. Anthony found them a secluded corner. The veiled woman revealed that she was Phoebe Phelps, mother of three and the wife of a Massachusetts senator. She and her thirteen-year-old daughter were hiding from her husband. Mrs. Phelps had complained that her husband beat her and that he entertained other women. Tired of her complaints, he accused her of suffering from delusions and had her committed to an insane asylum. He refused to let her see her children.

SUSAN B. ANTHONY

A husband in the nineteenth century, on his own authority, could have his wife committed to an insane asylum. Similarly, a father could have a daughter committed. The reverse was not true. A woman's word was not enough to prove that a man was insane. In many states, the only way a man could divorce his wife was to declare her insane and have her committed. Insane asylums in the nineteenth century were often brutal places. Elizabeth Cady Stanton, in her *Memoirs Reminiscences*, wrote, "Could the dark secrets of insane asylums be brought to light we would

Illustration showing how women in insane asylums were treated, from Packard's book

be shocked to know the great number of rebellious wives, sisters, and daughters who are thus sacrificed to false customs and barbarous laws made by men for women."

A woman taken to an asylum asking, "Is there no man in this crowd to protect a woman?" From a book written by Elizabeth Parsons Ware Packard called *Modern Persecutions or Insane Asylums Unveiled*. Packard's husband locked her in an asylum for years. She was fortunate enough to get a jury trial. The evidence against her was that she argued with her husband and flouted his authority. A jury found that she was sane, so she was released. Few women were able to obtain jury trials when committed to asylums.

★ ★ ★ ★ ★ ★ **SUSAN B. ANTHONY** ★ ★ ★ ★ ★ ★

Mrs. Phelps was locked in the asylum for seventeen months when at last her brother obtained a court order for her release on the grounds she was not insane. She wanted to visit her children, but her husband wouldn't allow it. She then turned to her brother for help. He told her, "The child belongs by law to the father and it is your place to submit. If you make any more trouble about it, we'll send you back to the asylum."

So Mrs. Phelps and her thirteen-year-old daughter ran away. They came to Albany because Mrs. Phelps read in the newspapers that she'd find Anthony there.

Anthony verified Mrs. Phelps's story, and then agreed to help her. They decided it would be easier for mother and daughter to hide in New York City, where they could blend into the crowds. So on Christmas Day 1860, while the nation was still reeling from the news that South Carolina had seceded from the Union, Mrs. Phelps, her daughter, and Anthony boarded a train for New York City. Once there, they visited Anthony's friends, until at last they found a friend and fellow abolitionist, Abigail Hopper Gibbons, who said she'd give Mrs. Phelps and her daughter temporary shelter, until more permanent arrangements could be made. Not long after, Mrs. Elizabeth F. Ellet, a well-known women's rights activist, placed Mrs. Phelps and her daughter with a doctor's

Civil War

family. The doctor later testified that Mrs. Phelps was sane. Mrs. Ellet found sewing work for Mrs. Phelps so she could pay for room and board for herself and her daughter.

Mr. Phelps soon learned that Anthony was hiding his wife and daughter. The law gave the father complete custody of the children, so he went to the police and accused Anthony of breaking the law by helping his runaway wife keep his child away from him. He threatened to have her arrested if she did not reveal the whereabouts of his wife and daughter. Word spread that Anthony had "abducted a man's child and must surrender it." Letters and telegrams poured in from all sides, urging her to reveal the whereabouts of mother and child. In Anthony's view, the law allowing a man to beat his wife, imprison her without cause, and prevent her from seeing her children degraded the woman to merchantable property. Her reply to those urging her to stop hiding Mrs. Phelps was that the laws were unjust, so submitting would be an "outrage." Therefore, she said, "I propose to defy the law and you also."

Anthony was by then widely known as one of the most active abolitionists, so the fact that she was illegally hiding a wife and child became a public scandal. At each stop along her lecture tour, she was mobbed by angry people demanding that she reveal the whereabouts of mother and child. Many of the male abolitionists were afraid Anthony's illegal actions would reflect badly on their antislavery work. William Lloyd Garrison wrote a pleading letter to Anthony not to get involved in "hasty and ill-judged" actions. Abolitionist Wendell Phillips wrote to her to insist that she return Mrs. Phelps to her husband. She wrote back, "All I have done is wholly right. Had I turned my back upon her I should have scorned myself . . . Trust me that as I ignore all law to help the slave, so will I ignore all to protect the enslaved woman."

William Lloyd Garrison, circa 1850. Photographed by Southworth and Hawes.

Anthony and Garrison met face-to-face at the antislavery convention in January. Garrison demanded, "Don't you know that the law of Massachusetts gives the father the entire guardianship and control of the children?"

"Yes, I know it," she told him. "Does not the law of the United States give the slaveholder the ownership of the slave? And don't you break it every time you help a slave to Canada? . . . You would die before you would deliver a slave to his master, and I will die before I will give up that child to its father."

Garrison was not persuaded, even though he claimed to believe in women's rights. It was clear to Anthony that even a man like Garrison, who considered himself liberal and open-minded and spent his life fighting for black freedom, might *say* he believed in women's rights, but he wasn't willing to help a beaten and abused runaway wife. To Anthony, this meant he believed women belonged under the dominion of men. She wrote in her diary that "Very many abolitionists have yet to learn the ABCs of women's rights."

Once, when Anthony was talking about the political and legal meaning of marriage for a woman, Reverend A. D. Mayo of Albany, New York, said, "You are not married, you have no business to be discussing marriage."

"Well, Mr. Mayo," she shot back, "you are not a slave, suppose you quit lecturing on slavery."

One of the few men who sided with Anthony on the Phelps matter was her father. While Daniel warned her not to "put a word on paper or make a statement to anyone that you are not prepared to face in court," he assured her that "legally you are wrong, but morally you are right, and I will stand by you."

Mr. Phelps didn't try to have Anthony arrested. She was too well known and too unpredictable. He knew she'd accuse him in public of abusing his wife, and he didn't want the bad publicity. Mr. Phelps stopped trying to wrest from Anthony the location of his wife and daughter, and instead hired detectives. It didn't take long for the detectives to locate them. One day, as his daughter was returning to her new home after Sunday school, he seized her and brought her back to his house. Mrs. Phelps tried to gain custody of her daughter, but the law was on her husband's side. Anthony responded by stepping up her campaign for laws that would give a mother legal rights to her children.

★ ★ ★ ★ ★ ★ ★ ★ ★ ★ ★ ★ ★ ★ ★

Anthony and several fellow abolitionists tried to hold a meeting in Buffalo in January 1861. With tensions rising between North and South, the newspapers accused Anthony of stirring up trouble and leading the nation into a bloody war. When she tried to take the stage, she was greeted with such hissing and booing that she couldn't speak. The mayor of Buffalo ordered the police to hold back the mobs so that the meeting could continue, but many of the police officers were proslavery and threw their support behind the rioters. Before the meeting could start, someone cut off the gas, leaving everyone in darkness and chaos. With the lights out, Anthony climbed up on the platform. She refused to budge until the lights were again turned on.

Anthony and her fellow reformers faced even worse in other towns. When they tried to meet in Syracuse, "Rotten eggs were thrown, benches broken, and knives and pistols gleamed in every direction." After sundown, effigies of Anthony and abolitionist Samuel May were carried through the city and burned by an angry mob. The meeting at Port Byron was broken up when members of a proslavery mob created an unbearable stink in the room by throwing cayenne pepper on the stove.

Anthony was met by a similar mob in Rome, New York. The mob rushed the stage, sang "The Star-Spangled Banner," and hooted. Later they followed her to her hotel in pursuit of the "damned abolitionists." The local newspaper, siding with the mob, called her a "pestiferous fanatic."

At a meeting in Auburn, Anthony showed her mettle when an angry mob stormed inside. At the height of the riot, according to a reporter on the scene, Anthony coolly leaned over the podium and said, "Why, boys, you're nothing but a *baby mob*, and you ought to go to Syracuse to learn how to do it, and also learn how to get before a Grand Jury."

★ ★ ★ ★ ★ ★ ★ ★ ★ ★ ★ ★ ★ ★ ★

One month after President Lincoln's inauguration, on April 12, 1861, the nation found itself plunged into a civil war when rebels in South Carolina fired on Fort Sumter. Lincoln responded by calling for seventy-five thousand volunteers to fight for the Union.

Many in the North clamored for an immediate end to the war, insisting on returning to "the Constitution as it is." They talked about "restoring our country to peace and prosperity." As always, Anthony had a response. "I ask you," she said to an audience, "what sort of peace, what sort of prosperity we had? Since the first slave-ship sailed up the James River with its human cargo and there . . . was sold to the highest bidder, we have had nothing but war . . . between the slave and the master there has been war, and war only, from the beginning."

To Anthony's great annoyance, Lincoln cast the war as being fought to save the Union, not to free the slaves. She understood he was afraid of angering the states along the border—Missouri,

Civil War

Delaware, Maryland, Kentucky, and West Virginia—which allowed slavery, but so far had not joined the Union or Confederacy. She believed his decision came from weakness. Her view of Lincoln was that he was a fearful and trembling leader. She believed he was prolonging the misery of those in bondage by not declaring the war to be about human freedom. "I wish the government would move quickly," she wrote in her diary, "proclaim freedom to every slave and call on every able-bodied negro to enlist in the Union army." That, she understood, would so strengthen the Union army that the rebellion—and the entire institution of slavery—would be snuffed out immediately. In her view, "To forever blot out slavery is the only possible compensation for this merciless war."

To her surprise, many of the most ardent abolitionists fell in line with Lincoln. Now that the war was on, Garrison and other abolition leaders didn't want to cause additional tension, so they took a "wait and see" attitude. Most northerners expected a quick Union victory. After all, the North controlled almost all the nation's heavy industry. Northerners outnumbered southerners. How hard could it be for the North to blockade and starve the South into submission? So that the entire North could focus on bringing about a swift victory, there was a loud clamor among the abolitionists for the women to stop agitating as well. They wanted the women to cancel their own meetings, including the National Women's Rights Convention planned for May of 1861.

Anthony vented her frustration to Lydia Mott. "All alike say, 'Have no conventions at this crisis! Wait until the war excitement abates' . . . All our reformers seem suddenly to have grown politic . . . Garrison, Phillips, Mrs. Mott, Mrs. Wright, Mrs. Stanton . . . I am sick at heart, but I can not carry the world against the wish and will of all our best friends." Seventeen hundred people had attended the 1859 women's rights convention, but now she couldn't find anyone willing to take the stage. She had no choice but to go along.

The following year, after the women disbanded and while the nation's attention was focused on the war, the New York legislature repealed the law that the women had worked so hard to get enacted, giving married women limited control of their own property.

"While the old guard sleeps, the young devils are wide-awake," Anthony said, fuming, "and we deserve to suffer for our confidence in 'man's sense of justice' and to have all we have gained thus snatched from us." Later, when Stanton understood the extent to which the decision to stop campaigning for women's rights during the war was a "blunder," she said, "ever since, I have taken my beloved Susan's judgment against the world."

With the women's conference called off and the abolitionists lying low, Anthony returned to the family farm in Rochester. She took up the burden of managing the farm so her father could go to Kansas to visit her brothers, who had moved west a few years earlier to help the abolition cause there. When her father returned, she spent her time taking care of Guelma, who had just had a baby.

Impressed by the sheer difficulty of giving birth and taking care of young children—and enraged by the second-class status of the women who managed it—Anthony wrote to Stanton, "Oh this babydom, what a constant, never-ending, all consuming strain! I realize more and more that child rearing should be looked upon as a profession which, like any other, must be made the primary work of those engaged in it." She came to feel that devaluing childcare and housework was part of how women were devalued and oppressed. A housewife cared for children and even produced goods used by the family—soap, candles, etc.—but her labors were not seen as the equivalent of a man's wage-earning work.

★★★★★★ SUSAN B. ANTHONY ★★★★★★

W hat happened next stunned the North: The Union Army suffered one humiliating defeat after another. The only major battle fought in 1861, the First Battle of Bull Run (Manassas)

Celebration of the Abolition of Slavery in the District of Columbia, by Frederick Dielman, *Harper's Weekly*, May 12, 1866

Civil War

in Virginia, ended in a humiliating defeat for the North. The only encouraging news for the Union came from the West, with General Ulysses S. Grant's victories in Tennessee in early 1862.

One full year after the war started, on April 3, 1862, Congress

✶ ✶ ✶ ✶ ✶ ✶ SUSAN B. ANTHONY ✶ ✶ ✶ ✶ ✶ ✶

at last passed the Compensated Emancipation Act freeing all of those enslaved in Washington, D.C. Lincoln signed the bill into law on April 16, 1862. Three months later, on July 17, Lincoln signed the Militia Act allowing blacks to serve in the Union Army.

That September, the North secured its first major victory in the Battle of Antietam, at Antietam Creek near Sharpsburg, Maryland. Immediately afterward, Lincoln announced that he was prepared to issue an Emancipation Proclamation freeing all those enslaved in the rebel states. Because of the president's limited powers, the Proclamation would have to be issued as an emergency war measure. It would not touch the slaves in the border states and it might easily be overturned by the Supreme Court or a future president—but it was an important symbol of the direction the Lincoln administration was heading.

✶ ✶ ✶ ✶ ✶ ✶ ✶ ✶ ✶ ✶ ✶ ✶ ✶ ✶ ✶

On a cold evening in November, during the height of the abolitionists' joy over the coming Emancipation Proclamation, Anthony was at home in Rochester. She and her father were sitting together, reading two of their abolition newspapers, the *National Anti-Slavery Standard* and the *Liberator*. They speculated about the effects of Lincoln's

Civil War

Emancipation Proclamation. Suddenly Daniel, who was then sixty-nine years old, doubled over with sharp stomach pains. His wife and daughters helped him to bed, where he lay for two weeks, in acute pain. There was nothing the doctors could do for him. He died on November 25, 1862.

With his death, Anthony "felt the foundations taken from beneath her feet." First she was "stunned and helpless," then her strength returned enough so that she could take charge of the funeral arrangements. All the leading abolitionists in the area came to pay their final respects to Daniel Anthony. Frederick Douglass delivered a eulogy. Two months later, Anthony talked of her father's death as "a shock not easily or soon to be recovered from."

7

Emancipation

"The principle of self-government cannot be violated with impunity. The individual's right to it is sacred—regardless of class, caste, race, color, sex or any other accident or incident of birth."
—*Susan B. Anthony*

Lincoln's Emancipation Proclamation went into effect on January 1, 1863. There was widespread rejoicing among abolitionists, and also fear that the Proclamation would be reversed by the proslavery Supreme Court, or overturned by a future president. So the reformers clamored for a Constitutional Amendment to permanently abolish slavery in America.

Anthony, who had long chaffed at being told to remain silent during the war, was eager to jump back into the public

Emancipation

arena to call for an antislavery amendment. She went to stay with Stanton, who by then had relocated with her family to New York City. The two women planned their strategy. They could not vote, so they had to find other ways to make their voice heard. Their plan was to organize a new group called the Women's National Loyal League for the sole purpose of pressuring Congress to get behind an amendment abolishing slavery. They would gather signatures for a petition. They planned a convention in New York in May, bringing women together to show their support for an antislavery amendment. They wrote an appeal titled "Call for a Meeting of the Loyal Women of the Nation," urging women to take a stand with the Union and black freedom.

At the first meeting of the Loyal League, the attendees voted on the resolution that the liberty and lives of "all slaves, all citizens of African descent, and all women are placed at the mercy of a legislation in which they are not represented . . . There can never be a true peace in this Republic until the civil and political equality of every subject of the government shall be practically established." A few of those present balked at entwining women's rights with black rights, but Anthony argued that the resolution was nothing more than a statement that "in a true democracy, in a genuine republic, every citizen who lives under the government must have the right of representation in that government."

The task of the Women's National Loyal League was: "Go to the rich, the poor, the high, the low, the soldier, the civilian, the white, the black; gather up the names of all who hate slavery, all who love liberty, and would have it in the law of the land, and lay them at the feet of Congress."

Armed with her mission, Anthony took to the lecture circuit. She implored the women in her audiences to

rise up with earnest, honest purpose and go forward in the way of right, fearless, as independent human beings . . . forget conventionalisms, forget what the world will say, whether you are in your place or out of it; think your best thoughts, speak your best words, do your best works, looking to your own consciences for approval.

Anthony's demand, that blacks must not only be freed, but also offered the full rights of citizenship, including the right to vote, was so radical in 1863 as to cause violent anger in many who heard it. In fact, the idea was so radical that her own brother Daniel would not allow the opinion into his liberal newspaper for fear of offending too many readers.

Emancipation

Anthony dedicated every waking hour to the Loyal League, pressing every able-bodied woman she could into service, writing letters, giving lectures, spreading the word. With her confidence growing, she stopped reading prepared speeches. Instead she spoke from notes and engaged more directly with her audiences. Her speeches became more riveting, and she earned a reputation as a charismatic and effective leader. The young women who came in contact with her felt inspired, infused with the feeling that they, too, could step forward and make a difference.

At each lecture, Anthony asked her audience to support her work by offering a donation beyond the small fee they'd paid for admission. Her appeals worked. As long as she lived and traveled frugally, she was able to support her travels and her work. The first time that abolitionist William Lloyd Garrison heard her plea for money, he said, "Well, Miss Anthony, you're the most audacious beggar I ever heard."

✱ ✱ ✱ ✱ ✱ ✱ ✱ ✱ ✱ ✱ ✱ ✱ ✱ ✱

Anthony had seen angry mobs before, but never before had she seen the anger and violence that erupted in New York City on July 15, 1863, when Lincoln signed the Draft Act into law, allowing able-bodied African American men to be drafted

Emancipation

into the Union Army. Violent riots broke out all over the city. Some whites started to blame the Civil War on African American demands for freedom. They rioted, and turned on innocent blacks and murdered them. A black orphanage was destroyed. It has been estimated that as many as twelve hundred people were killed.

"These are terrible times," Anthony wrote in a letter to her mother and sister. Two days later, when the military arrived and brought back a semblance of order, Anthony was back on the stage, demanding black equality.

✶ ✶ ✶ ✶ ✶ ✶ ✶ ✶ ✶ ✶ ✶ ✶ ✶ ✶ ✶

The Loyal League, with Anthony and Stanton at the helm, gathered one hundred thousand signatures in nine months, making it the largest ever recorded in history. On February 9, 1864, Massachusetts senator Charles Sumner presented the petitions to the Senate, lavishing praise on the women for noble work, calling them "a mighty army, one hundred thousand strong, without arms or banners." Two months later, the Senate passed the Thirteenth Amendment declaring that

"The Riots at New York—the rioters burning and sacking the colored orphan asylum," *Harper's Weekly*, August 1, 1863

Neither slavery nor involuntary servitude, except as a punishment for crime whereof the party shall have been duly convicted, shall exist within the United States, or any place subject to their jurisdiction.

Congress shall have power to enforce this article by appropriate legislation.

The amendment next went to the House of Representatives, where it was defeated by the proslavery majority. So Anthony and the volunteers of the Loyal League, now numbering about two thousand, went back to gathering names on a petition. By the end of the year, they had secured an additional three hundred thousand signatures.

Also by the end of the year, the war turned decidedly in favor of the North, with the Union Army scoring victories at Gettysburg, in the Mississippi Valley, and Georgia. Riding the wave of military victory, Lincoln ran for reelection on a promise to secure the unconditional surrender of the South. His opponent, northern Democrat George B. McClellan, ran on a "peace" platform, promising to negotiate peace with the South. McClellan's plan would put an immediate end to the war—while keeping slavery intact. Lincoln feared that the war-weary North would find the

Emancipation

idea of instant peace irresistible and would elect McClellan. But with the Union Army's continued success, and with the Confederate states not participating in the election, Lincoln won with 55.4 percent of the popular vote.

Meanwhile, a change in attitude was sweeping over voters in the North and West. Before the war, many voters believed that compromising over slavery would hold the Union together. Before and during the Civil War, a majority of voters blamed the troubles on the abolitionists for stirring unrest. Now it was obvious to many that it was the institution of slavery breaking up the Union, and as long as slavery existed anywhere, there would be division and anger.

Emboldened and empowered by his reelection and the changing tide of public opinion, Lincoln threw his weight behind the Thirteenth Amendment. With pressure from Lincoln and the public, proslavery Congressmen began changing their minds and saying they would vote for the amendment. There were also rumors, followed by actual evidence, that some Republicans in the administration were doling out favors in exchange for a few much-needed votes.

On January 31, 1865, a slim majority in the House of Representatives passed the Thirteenth Amendment, abolishing slavery.

★★★★★★ SUSAN B. ANTHONY ★★★★★★

Senator Charles Sumner credited the Women's Loyal League as a "principle force behind the drive for the Thirteenth Amendment." What was needed now, for the amendment to become part of the Constitution, was ratification by three-quarters of the states.

★ ★ ★ ★ ★ ★ ★ ★ ★

Daniel Read Anthony, date and photographer unknown

Anthony wasn't among the crowds of women who wept and cheered in the House gallery when the vote was taken. Her newly married brother Daniel and his wife, Anna, had been begging her to come to Kansas for a visit. (Her youngest brother, Merritt, had by then moved back to New York State, and got married there.) So earlier in January, with her work on the petitions finished, she boarded a westbound train for Leavenworth, Kansas.

As the owner of the respected newspaper, the *Leavenworth Bulletin,* Daniel frequently entertained distinguished guests.

Emancipation

Anthony was at ease living with her brother and sister-in-law, and was soon working to help the former slaves who were flocking to Kansas. She worked for programs offering job training and instruction in reading and writing. She sought ways to integrate the new arrivals into schools, including Sunday schools. Living in Kansas brought her closer to the Indian wars, of which she heartily disapproved. She declared it cruel to retain the Seventh Kansas Regiment for the purpose of going out to the plains to fight the Native people.

When her brother was nominated to run for mayor and the campaign took much of his time, she helped out by running his newspaper for him. His only request was that she not have it *all* women's rights and Negro suffrage. She learned that she disliked writing for publication. Instead she mostly read the news exchanges, clipped what she thought was newsworthy, and put it into the *Leavenworth Bulletin*. Her talents were in organization and management. She ran her brother's newspaper like clockwork.

She tried to hire a black printer, but the rest of the labor force protested by going on strike. She was furious. In her diary, she wrote that it was a "burning, blistering shame" that the other workers made it impossible for her to hire a black man—but there was nothing she could do other than try to find him another job.

SUSAN B. ANTHONY

She was unable to find him a job using his skills, so he had to work as a common laborer.

From the newspapers and from letters, she learned that the abolitionists had split into two factions. One side, led by William Lloyd Garrison, felt their objective in passing the Thirteenth Amendment had been accomplished, so the group should disband. Others of her friends, most notably Frederick Douglass and Wendell Phillips, disagreed, believing that abolishing slavery was not enough. They argued that if the freed slaves were not granted constitutional protection, there would be nothing to stop their former masters from passing laws forcing them into a condition as oppressive as slavery. Anthony, naturally enough, sided with Douglass and Phillips.

Anthony was still in Kansas on April 9, 1865, when Confederate general Lee surrendered to Union general Ulysses Grant, bringing the Civil War to a close. Six days later, she recorded in her diary:

Morning telegram reported President Lincoln assassinated at Fords Theatre in Washington . . . Vice President Johnson immediately sworn in.

Emancipation

One day in early August, she was sitting in her brother's offices reading the newspapers when she learned that there was talk of another amendment guaranteeing all *men* the right to vote, regardless of race. She left the newspaper office, went to her brother's house, and began making arrangements to return to New York. She intended to fight this outrage. To get the money to travel back to the East Coast, she worked out a deal with the *National Anti-Slavery Standard* to earn her train fare by making speeches along the way and collecting subscriptions to the newspaper.

Wendell Phillips, photographed by Charles D. Fredericks, published 1865

She was preparing for her journey when Stanton sent her a frantic message: "I have argued constantly with Phillips and the whole fraternity, but I fear one and all will favor enfranchising the Negro without us. Woman's cause is in deep water."

Abolitionist Wendell Phillips had recently written to Stanton, asking her to continue putting women's suffrage on hold while they worked to obtain votes for blacks. He also gave a speech at an Anti-Slavery Society meeting advocating a constitutional amendment offering the vote to all persons regardless of race, condition, or color. He then said, "I hope some day to be bold enough to add 'sex.' However, my friends, we must take up but one question at a time, and this hour belongs exclusively to the Negro."

Stanton was appalled and enraged. She'd thought that after all the women had done to support Republican causes, and after demonstrating their political abilities, their fellow Republicans would support women's right to vote. Both she and Anthony also understood that, having remained silent for so long about women's claims, it would be "impertinent" to raise the issue now.

To Phillips, Stanton shot back a short letter:

Dear Friend,—may I ask in reply to your fallacious letter just one question based on the apparent opposition in which you place the Negro and the woman? My question is this: Do you believe the African race is composed entirely of males?

To Anthony, she wrote, "Come back and help. There will be a room for you."

8
We the People

"It was we the people; not we, the white male citizens; nor yet we, the male citizens; but we, the whole people, who formed the Union."
—*Susan B. Anthony*

Anthony's mother and sister Mary no longer lived on the farm. Lucy was advancing in age, and Mary's time was so taken up with commuting to her teaching job that they couldn't manage the farm themselves. So they sold the farm and moved in with Guelma and her husband, who were renting a charming two-story Italianate-style house on Madison Street in Rochester. The following year, Lucy bought the house they were all living in.

When Anthony alighted from the train in Rochester, she had

no carriage money. She'd earned her train fare, but had nothing left over, so she walked the rest of the way home. She didn't stay long, though. Soon she was on her way to New York, to Stanton's house, where the two women got right to work, drafting speeches, writing letters and articles, getting in touch with sympathetic politicians, and planning their strategy for making sure that any suffrage amendments included guarantees for women.

Meanwhile, more and more states were ratifying the Thirteenth Amendment. A number of the states in the former Confederacy ratified the amendment because they understood that slavery as it existed before the Civil War was over, and they believed if they ratified the amendment, the federal government would leave them alone. On December 6, 1865, when Georgia became the twenty-seventh state to ratify the amendment, it became part of the Constitution, permanently abolishing slavery in the United States.

As soon as the Thirteenth Amendment became law, Mississippi and South Carolina enacted laws called the Black Codes to restrict the liberty of the newly freed slaves. Other states soon followed. While the Black Codes varied somewhat from state to state, the codes generally required blacks to sign yearly labor contracts and made vagrancy—or homelessness—a crime. Blacks

Illustration of a man who violated the Black Codes, could not pay the fine, and was forced into labor to cover the fine. The Black Codes began a history of enacting criminal laws that targeted black people, and thus gave rise to prisons with a disproportionately large percentage of black inmates.

who left their masters but refused to sign labor contracts were arrested, convicted as vagrants, and forced into labor as convicts. The Black Codes also prevented blacks from attending public schools, entering certain professions, serving on juries, or testifying in court against whites.

The Thirteenth Amendment made an exception for those convicted of crimes, allowing convicts to be forced into labor, so southern law enforcement found pretexts for arresting and convicting black men, chaining them up, and putting them to work in chain gangs. In the words of Frederick Douglass, many of the freed blacks were "enclosed in the same dark dungeon" they had been in slavery.

Stories coming out of the South were terrifying. Free blacks were subject to whippings and lynchings if they failed to acknowledge white superiority. On May 1, 1866, an angry mob in Memphis opened fire on unarmed black soldiers. In New Orleans, where a group of blacks gathered to demand the vote, thirty-four black men and women were slaughtered. Nurse Clara Barton, founder of the American Red Cross, reported that there were thousands of hungry black men, women, and children at the door, and thousands more trembling in fear, all over the South, surrounded by enemies who believed blacks must remain in bondage.

In January of 1866, Ohio congressman John Bingham presented the Fourteenth Amendment to Congress. Section I of the amendment guaranteed citizenship to any person born in the United States, which would instantly transform all the former slaves into citizens. Section I then went on to guarantee all "persons" the "privileges and immunities" of citizenship, and "equal protection" of the laws:

We the People

No state shall make or enforce any law which shall abridge the privileges or immunities of citizens of the United States; nor shall any state deprive any person of life, liberty, or property, without due process of law; nor deny to any person within its jurisdiction the equal protection of the laws.

. . . The Congress shall have power to enforce, by appropriate legislation, the provisions of this article.

This was exactly what Anthony and the other reformers had been fighting for. It was breathtaking and essentially rewrote entire portions of the Constitution. Thus far in America's history, each state had unfettered rights in how it treated people living within its borders. This short passage restructured the American government, taking power from the states, and giving the federal government authority to regulate any local customs or laws that violated the rights of its citizens.

The problem came in Section II, which referred to voters as the "male inhabitants of each state . . . being twenty-one years of age." Because each state's number of congressmen was proportional to the population, Section II was intended to penalize states that did not allow black men to vote by reducing their numbers of representatives.

★★★★★ SUSAN B. ANTHONY ★★★★★

Stanton and Anthony seized on the significance of the word "male." Stanton said, "If that word 'male' be inserted, it will take us a century at least to get it out." Stanton, Anthony, and others, frantic, persuaded Thaddeus Stevens of Pennsylvania—one of the most liberal congressmen—to present a petition from the women for universal suffrage, asking that women be included. He presented the petition, but it was promptly rejected by the Committee on the Judiciary.

Universal Suffrage petition submitted to Congress in 1866, and immediately rejected

The eleventh National Women's Rights Convention was held on May 10, 1866, in the Church of the Puritans in Union Square in New York City. Many of the brightest lights in the abolition and women's rights movement attended: Ernestine Rose, Lucretia Mott, Frederick Douglass, Martha Wright, and others. Also there was Wendell Phillips, who frequently attended women's rights

We the People

meetings, and had always declared himself in favor of equal rights for women.

Stanton and Anthony hoped to repair their rift with Phillips, but alas that was obviously not going to happen. When it was Phillips's turn to speak, he took the floor and announced that because "woman" was "in thrall to fashion" (by which he meant women cared only about superficial things, like clothing and fashion) the ballot would be worthless to her. He blamed the Confederate uprising on southern women, who he said were "corrupting the channels of politics." He then asked if women wanted power, why didn't they try to earn money? There was nothing on the statute books to forbid gainful employment. "No ballot box will help you," he told the women. "Go home and reform yourselves."

If he thought women were as free to earn money as men, he

> **WOMAN'S RIGHTS.**
>
> Eleventh National Convention of the Strong Minded Females.
>
> The Ballot for Women, White and Black, the Crowning Right of Civilization.
>
> **A GREAT WOMAN'S RIGHTS PETITION**
>
> Phillips, Beecher and Tilton on the Woman's Rights Question.
>
> Spirited Speeches by Elizabeth Cady Stanton, Lucretia Mott, Susan B. Anthony and Others.
> &c. &c. &c.
>
> The mental giants among the females of this country, together with a fair proportion of the physically able-

The *New York Herald* announced the 1866 convention of "strong minded females"—the meeting at which the Equal Rights Association was formed. To Anthony's dismay, more men attended than women.

obviously wasn't paying attention. The other speakers were less divisive, and the group realized they were in more agreement than conflict. Nobody was happy with the amendment as it was written. Abolitionists like Frederick Douglass were unhappy because the amendment fell short of guaranteeing black men the right to vote, and hence did not achieve equal rights. The women were unhappy because they were excluded from Section II.

Anthony took the floor and proposed that the two movements—black freedom and women's suffrage—merge into a new organization called the American Equal Rights Association. Now that the slaves had been emancipated, she pointed out, women and blacks shared the same legal status: citizens without equal rights, including the right to vote. Her argument was that two separate movements would require double cost of time and money. The group, she proposed, should focus on "one grand, distinctive, national idea—Universal Suffrage."

The group adopted her resolution. Anthony then nominated Stanton as president. Anthony was the workhorse, but with Quaker humility and a natural distaste for any hierarchy, she had no desire for a title. Stanton was elected president. The group also voted to oppose any language that excluded women.

Phillips may have been outvoted at the Equal Rights

Association meeting, but he wasn't backing down. He and Anthony exchanged angry words about a month later at a meeting held in the office of the *National Anti-Slavery Standard*. Phillips, still insisting that black men should be given the vote but not women, told Anthony that women would have to wait at least a generation for the right to vote. Anthony replied that she would rather "cut off her right hand than ask the ballot for the black man and not for woman."

Before long, Anthony was able to present a petition to Congress with ten thousand signatures pleading for women to be included. Republican senator Charles Sumner—the same senator who had heaped praise on the women for driving the Thirteenth Amendment—shrugged off the petition as "most inopportune."

Several prominent Republican politicians tried to mollify Stanton and Anthony with assurances that "The insertion of that word [male] puts up no new barrier against woman," so, "do not embarrass us but wait until we get the Negro question settled." These politicians also pointed out that there was nothing in the Fourteenth Amendment to prevent individual states from allowing women to vote, should they choose to.

This failed to reassure the women. They knew that amending the Constitution was a cumbersome process, and passing amendments did not happen often. In fact, the Thirteenth Amendment was the first time the Constitution had been amended since 1804. If the moment passed, who knew how long it might take before the door to an amendment was opened again?

✶ ✶ ✶ ✶ ✶ ✶ ✶ ✶ ✶ ✶ ✶ ✶ ✶ ✶

On June 18, 1866, Congress adopted the amendment as proposed. To force the states in the former Confederacy to ratify the Fourteenth Amendment, Congress required ratification before they'd be allowed to send senators and representatives back to Congress. Getting the former Confederate states to do the bidding of the North was helped by the Second Reconstruction Act, which, among other things, required that black men be given the right to vote in new elections to be supervised by the military. Thousands of southern government officials were removed from office and replaced with Union officers and blacks newly released from the bonds of slavery. Bowing to pressure, on July 9, 1868, South Carolina became the twenty-first state to ratify the Fourteenth Amendment.

It was soon obvious that the Fourteenth Amendment's penalty for not allowing black men to vote wasn't enough. States still refused to enfranchise black men, so there was talk of a Fifteenth

Amendment guaranteeing that right to black men. Anthony and Stanton insisted that if an amendment guaranteed black men the right to vote, women, too, must be included.

Wendell Phillips and others renewed their claim that the time was not ripe for women to be given the right to vote. Phillips set out to persuade the women that it was their "duty" to "sacrifice their own claims and devote themselves to securing suffrage for the colored men."

If he was deliberately trying to choose words to enrage Anthony, he couldn't have done a better job. Anthony believed the source of women's oppression was the very notion, promulgated by men, that women must dutifully sacrifice themselves for others. At an antislavery meeting in Philadelphia, Anthony, as spokesperson for the women, begged Phillips to reconsider his position. She asked him whether here, in the presence of the women who had stood shoulder to shoulder with him in all his hard-fought battles of the past twenty years—would he really abandon them now?

Phillips repeated that the women must step aside. He obviously expected them to obey. When they did not, he pushed back, insisting that including women would jeopardize the Fifteenth Amendment if they insisted on being included. It was clear to

Anthony that the Republicans in Congress had the power to push amendments through. The Thirteenth and Fourteenth Amendments, which were so radical that five years earlier they would have been deemed impossible, were proof. Anthony believed that if the men in power wanted to add women's suffrage to the amendment, they could.

When Stanton and Anthony still refused to back down, Phillips found a way to cut off some of their funding. He controlled the purse for the funds left by donor Francis Jackson, and he found pretext for denying the women their share.

The second annual meeting of the American Equal Rights Association was held on May 9, 1867. Over the years, Anthony had developed a friendship with Sojourner Truth, who often stayed in the Anthony family home during her travels. Truth made clear that if the battle was between black men and women, she was firmly on the side of women. So Anthony invited Truth to speak at the meeting. Lucretia Mott and Robert Purvis presided. Truth, who was then eighty years old, took the stage and said, "There is a great stir about colored men getting their rights, but not a word about the colored women; and if colored men get their rights and not colored women theirs, you see the colored men will be masters over the women, and it will be just as bad as it was before."

We the People

Lest there be any doubt, Truth elaborated on what she meant. "[Colored women] go out washing," she explained, "which is about as high as a colored woman gets, and their men go about idle, strutting up and down; and when the women come home, they ask for their money and take it all, and then scold you because there is no food . . . I want women to have their rights. In the courts women have no right, no voice; nobody speaks for them."

Reformers began to take sides: Should only black men get the vote, or should women—black and white—get the vote, too? African American reformer Charles Remond—who had traveled and worked closely with Anthony in the American Anti-Slavery Society—sided with Anthony and Stanton. "All I ask for myself," he said, "I claim for my wife and sister. Let our actions be based on the rock of everlasting principle." Scholar and former slave Robert Purvis also sided with Anthony and Stanton, saying,

Charles Lenox Remond, circa 1851–1855, photographed by Samuel Broadbent

SUSAN B. ANTHONY

I am an anti-slavery man because I hate tyranny and in my nature revolt against oppression whatever its form and character. As an Abolitionist, therefore, I am for the equal rights movement, and as one of the confessedly oppressed race, how could I be otherwise? With what grace could I ask the women of this country to labor for my enfranchisement, and at the same time be unwilling to put forth a hand to remove the tyranny, in some respects greater, to which they are subjected?

Purvis also struck fear into Stanton's heart with his prediction that if black men were enfranchised but women were not, the black men would "give their influence like a dead weight against the equality of women."

Most of the reformers though, black and white, lined up behind Wendell Phillips. Frederick Douglass quietly sided against the women, arguing that black rights were more pressing than women's rights. Lucy Stone—who had always been one of the most radical and outspoken women's rights reformers—wrote that there were tears in her eyes and a nail went through her breast when she realized the abolitionists were turning their backs on the women. Nonetheless Stone would willingly step aside for the black men, "thankful in my soul if *any*body can get out of this black pit." Frances Ellen Watkins Harper, an African American poet and novelist, regretted that the nation could not handle two questions at once, votes for black men and women. She said she was willing to put rights for black men ahead of women. In just a few years, though, Harper would look back with a different opinion. In 1873, she reflected back and saw the time after the Civil War as the time when "the colored man vaulted into power, and the colored woman was left to serve." She also said, "As much as white women need the ballot, colored women need it more."

Lucy Stone, photographed by G. W. Bartlett, 1853. Stone, an early women's rights advocate, startled the nation when she refused to take her husband's name. As a result, independent women were often called "Lucy Stoners."

Frances Ellen Watkins Harper, a poet, novelist, and women's rights advocate. Photographer and year unknown.

SUSAN B. ANTHONY

> The Founding Fathers assumed that the government would remain mostly in the hands of educated, landowning men partly on the theory that a person with a stake in government could be trusted to vote wisely, and on the theory that a man who owned property could exercise independent judgment because he didn't answer to a master or superior. Education was deemed important for voters to be able to make informed decisions. During the

In December of 1866, Senator Edgar Cowan took the Senate floor. He was a Republican from Pennsylvania who was also a conservative and white supremacist. Using Anthony's argument that all people should be equal, he said he preferred that *neither* black men *nor* women get the ballot, but if the black men were to vote, how could the women be excluded? He warned his colleagues that if they enfranchised black men without women, "Mrs. Elizabeth Cady Stanton, Mrs. Frances Dana Gage, and Miss Susan B. Anthony are on your heels."

Conservative Republicans like Cowan and Democrats who argued that women should be allowed to vote never explicitly stated their reasons. Stanton believed their reason was arithmetic.

We the People

> years immediately following the Revolutionary War, most states limited voting eligibility to property-owning men.
>
> Throughout the early nineteenth century, states gradually expanded voting rights to all white men, whether or not they were educated and whether or not they owned property. By the time of the Civil War, all white men, regardless of whether they were literate, could vote. With the exception of certain local elections in Kentucky, no women could vote.

As one politician pointed out, "Four million Southern women will counterbalance four million Negro men and women." If women *and* black men were enfranchised, the Republicans would be no better off in national elections because southern white women would vote Democrat. On the other hand, if only black men were enfranchised, Republicans would gain millions of voters who, unlike southern women, would vote for the party of Lincoln.

Stanton believed that the Republicans were about to sacrifice women's rights on the altar of political expediency. Anthony, in contrast, believed Republican men didn't want women to vote simply because they didn't want to give up their dominance over women.

9

Betrayal

*"Cautious, careful people always
casting about to preserve their reputations
can never effect a reform."*
— *Susan B. Anthony*

In March of 1867, the Kansas state legislature approved two initiatives: one to allow blacks to vote and another to allow women to vote. The initiatives now needed approval from the voters—all of whom, of course, were white and male. Lucy Stone and other reformers had visited Kansas and spoke there. Republicans constituted a majority of the population. It seemed like a place to score a win.

So Anthony and Stanton headed west. By the time they arrived, Kansas was already a minefield. Democrats were raising

Betrayal

racist fears to scare people into not wanting blacks to have the right to vote. Republicans split. A group of conservative Republicans refused to endorse the initiative for women to vote, and in fact, actively campaigned against women's suffrage, raising fears that if women were allowed to vote, traditional family life would fall apart. One of the Republican anti-woman speakers asked audiences if they really wanted "every old maid to vote." The other faction of more liberal Republicans backed both initiatives, but they were disorganized, lacked resources, and, in Anthony's view, didn't put much energy into promoting either initiative.

Anthony could see that certain politicians were trying to pit the women against the black men, hoping the infighting would sink both causes. One newspaper editor saw the same thing and reported that the black men were eager for the vote, and "their pretended champions have poured such stuff into their ears, until they have begun to think the female suffrage people are their worst enemies."

Anthony did her best to "squelch the black-versus-women story." When she spoke to large groups of African Americans, she told the men they must "stop asking about equal rights for themselves but must include their wives and daughters also." The women in the audience would burst into foot-stomping applause.

SUSAN B. ANTHONY

Because Phillips had cut off Anthony's funding, she was so strapped for cash that she was unable to pay speakers and had to scratch together the money for her own day-to-day expenses. She was able to persuade the governor of Kansas to drive her to events, which helped draw crowds.

Anthony could see that the majority was against her. Two weeks before the election, the situation seemed hopeless. That was when George Francis Train, a notorious and vulgar Democrat, burst onto the scene. Anthony believed that Train had been invited to Kansas by the St. Louis suffragists to help with the women's campaign. Historian Kathleen Barry, in combing through correspondence from the era, determined that Train had been invited by Henry Blackwell, husband of women's rights reformer Lucy Stone. Blackwell entered into an agreement with Samuel Newitt Wood, a Republican lawmaker in Kansas, to bring Train to Kansas. Blackwell and Wood believed that Train would persuade enough Democrats to

George Francis Train, circa 1856. Photographer unknown.

Betrayal

vote for women's suffrage so that the measure would succeed. The plan backfired spectacularly.

Train was wealthy and a magnetic speaker, with an outsized personality, commanding attention wherever he went. He declared himself in favor of women's suffrage. He imagined himself a renegade outsider, and hoped one day to run for president of the United States. Born in Massachusetts, he'd been proslavery before the war. After the war started, he switched sides and became a Unionist, but he held on to his belief that the blacks were an inferior race. Republicans called him a racist—which he was. They also called him a lunatic. Train urged the Democrats to do their duty and vote for the women's suffrage initiative. He was not in favor of blacks voting, and said so in extremely offensive terms.

On election day, both initiatives—the one for women and the one for black men—were soundly defeated. Train apparently lost more Republican voters than he gained Democratic ones. The conservative faction of Republicans claimed that they lost the initiative to give black men the vote because it was "loaded down" by the "side issue" of women's suffrage—even though, as Anthony knew, they'd never put serious effort into getting the vote for black men. Anthony could see they were just scapegoating the women. Frederick Douglass blamed Train and what he considered the worthless Republicans in Kansas (who he still preferred to the Democrats). Blaming Train, or even Anthony and Stanton, was unfounded because, that same year, black suffrage initiatives lost in other states where there had been no George Francis Train or women seeking their rights.

Nonetheless people blamed the women. Anthony and Stanton blamed their loss on former allies, particularly Wendell Phillips, who refused to support them. Anthony tried to spin the defeat as a win. Nine thousand votes had been cast in favor of women's suffrage. She argued that nine thousand was a good place to start.

With the election over, Train offered Anthony and Stanton start-up funds for a women's rights newspaper. A newspaper, like money, was power. It meant having a voice. No longer would Anthony have to trudge around to other people's newspaper offices hoping to get a notice posted.

Anthony and Stanton accepted his offer, scandalizing many of their Republican allies and associates back east, who were indignant that they would continue associating with a man such as Train. Among the more notable finger-pointers was Henry Blackwell, who smeared Anthony and Stanton for associating with Train while hiding the fact that he had initially invited Train to Kansas.

Betrayal

Blackwell, like Phillips, seemed to expect Anthony and Stanton to follow his direction. When he approved of the women working with Train, they could. But when he said stop, he expected them to stop. One historian concluded that the male abolitionists had already decided to abandon the women's cause, and Anthony and Stanton's decision to take money from a notorious racist like Train—and even continue sharing a stage with him—gave them a reason to denounce Anthony and Stanton publicly.

Anthony believed the men were angry because Train's money would empower the women. As she saw the situation, when the Republican Party and male abolitionists abandoned the women, she was left with three options: She could follow Wendell Phillips's orders and meekly step aside, or she could try to achieve political victory without any funding—a near impossibility—or she could accept help from Train, which would give her a "fighting chance" to score a victory for women.

With start-up funds from Train and the promise of more money later, Stanton and Anthony returned to New York to establish their newspaper. Anthony became the business manager in charge of fund-raising, renting office space, selling subscriptions, and tracking down advertisers. Stanton did the writing and editing. Initially Stanton had a coeditor, abolitionist Parker Pillsbury. They called

★ ★ ★ ★ ★ ★ SUSAN B. ANTHONY ★ ★ ★ ★ ★ ★

The Revolution.

PRINCIPLE, NOT POLICY; JUSTICE, NOT FAVORS.

VOL. I.—NO. 1.   NEW YORK, WEDNESDAY, JANUARY 8, 1868. $2.00 A YEAR.

Masthead of the first issue of the *Revolution*, New York, January 8, 1868

their paper the *Revolution*. On the masthead was the motto: "Principle, not policy; Justice, not favors." Later, they would add "Men their rights, nothing more. Women their rights, nothing less."

Stanton knew how to gain attention for the newspaper with publicity stunts like getting President Andrew Johnson to subscribe. Publication of their newspaper established Stanton and Anthony as national figures.

Anthony and Stanton's association with Train turned out to be short-lived. Early in 1866, Train left for England, where he was arrested in Dublin for encouraging Irish independence. He remained in jail for a full year, and sent them no more money, so all they had from him were the start-up funds. They were on their own, raising their own money to sustain their newspaper by selling subscriptions and advertisements.

Stanton used their newspaper to take shots at Wendell Phillips, William Lloyd Garrison, and Phillips's newspaper, the

Betrayal

National Anti-Slavery Standard, for refusing to get behind women's suffrage. "Mr. Garrison always was," she wrote, "and probably always will be as imperious as Caesar toward those who do not see all things through his spectacles." In abandoning the cause of women, she accused him of being "despotic in spirit and purpose."

Garrison was shocked. It was the kind of thing he himself had done with his political adversaries, but he evidently didn't expect such behavior from a woman. He fought back, declaring that the fact that Anthony and Stanton took money from a racist was clear evidence that Anthony and Stanton had abandoned all their principles. Stanton and Anthony were not intimidated, nor deterred, by such attacks.

Now that they had their own newspaper, they took up any causes in which they believed women were unjustly treated. Anthony was particularly concerned with the plight of female factory workers, who were working under increasingly oppressive conditions. In 1868, she called meetings of female factory workers to talk about working conditions and the need for them to receive fair pay. She held the meetings in tenement buildings where factory girls lived. She opened the meetings by asking about the working conditions. The women—many of them still in their teens—showed their scratches, bruises, and blisters. One

SUSAN B. ANTHONY

woman described how she worked three days on an extra project for which the boss refused to pay her.

Anthony formed a Working Women's Association to protect the female factory workers and demand that they receive the same pay as the men. The association met in the offices of the *Revolution*. Anthony's goal was for the newly formed National Labor Union to recognize the special needs of women workers, in particular the lower pay and the harassment that women in factories were subjected to. The *Revolution* supported the National Labor Union's call for an eight-hour workday and the unionizing of workers.

Many of Anthony's fellow reformers were distressed that she was treading into the controversial issue of labor unions. They believed that getting involved in such causes would take the focus away from women's suffrage.

They were even more scandalized by some of the articles and opinions Stanton published in the *Revolution*. Stanton discussed the hypothetical: If only one group, women or black men, should get the vote first, which should it be? She argued that it should be women, because women were superior to men. On December 24, 1868, she delivered a blistering attack on men. She said enfranchising black men and not women would strengthen the horrors resulting from a "man's government" by adding two million votes from the brutal half of humanity. "We object to the amendment of the Constitution of the United States securing Manhood Suffrage," because "there is only one safe, sure way to build a government, and that is on the equality of all citizens, male and female, black and white." The Fifteenth Amendment, "exalting the son over the mother who bore him," amounted to "subjugating everywhere moral power to brute force."

The problem, Stanton argued, was the nature of men. "The male element, already too much in the ascendant, is a destructive force; stern, selfish, aggrandizing; loving war, violence, conquest, acquisition; breeding discord, disorder, disease, and death." She surveyed humanity's history of war and discord, laid the blame on the nature of men, and argued that the only way to balance such impulses was to enfranchise women.

She stood on its head the old argument that women needed to stay out of politics because they were too pure for such messy business, arguing that men had created the mess, so women—who were purer and kinder—should enter the arena to clean it. "Men need refining," Stanton wrote. "Let woman fulfill her God-like mission. She is nobler, purer, better than man."

Stanton stirred the pot by denouncing the very idea that "educated women" should step back while "two million largely illiterate and ignorant" men newly released from the bonds of slavery should have the vote ahead them, and hence the power to make laws that women must obey. As if that wasn't harsh enough, she said that giving black men power over women (both white and black) would "culminate in fearful outrages on womanhood, especially in Southern states."

Scholars have been divided over whether Stanton's remarks were fundamentally anti-male, with black men being a subset of men, or whether her remarks were fundamentally anti-black. Stanton's accusers point out that many of her remarks were tinged with racial stereotypes about black men, and that her own privileged family background suggested elitism. She certainly believed that she had earned the right to vote because of her own superior education, and because she had proven herself as capable as any man in the political arena, and she believed herself more capable of voting wisely than the millions of uneducated and illiterate men newly released from bondage.

Stanton's defenders point out that she had always worked for black freedom and equality, and in firing off her *Revolution* articles, she was reacting to being told that women must do their duty and graciously step aside while yet another group of men were given political dominance over them. She was also speaking to people

Betrayal

in her own social circles, none of whom, at the time, genuinely believed Stanton was a racist, even while they expressed shock at her behavior. To take one example, while calling Stanton out for refusing to step aside for black men, Frederick Douglass reminded his audience that "when there were few houses in which the black man could have put his head, this woolly head of mine found refuge in the house of Mrs. Elizabeth Cady Stanton."

By that point, Anthony and Stanton didn't care who they offended. In the words of one scholar, "These two women were determined to ride roughshod over obstacles, ignore critics, and take help wherever they could get it because Kansas left them with an urgent sense that woman suffrage should have been won *yesterday*."

✦ ✦ ✦ ✦ ✦ ✦ ✦ ✦ ✦ ✦ ✦ ✦ ✦ ✦ ✦

Anthony was grateful for her small victories. That year, as she did each year, she returned to the New York State Teachers' Convention, where she tirelessly chipped away at the rules and procedures. In 1856, she broke ground by receiving permission to deliver a paper on the value of educating girls alongside boys. Because she continually insisted on speaking, eventually other women, too, stood up to speak. By the end of the

SUSAN B. ANTHONY

At about this time, the North Carolina Supreme Court decided a wife-beating case. In 1868, in Wilkes County, North Carolina, Elizabeth Rhodes grew tired of her husband beating her, so she filed charges against him. At the trial, she presented evidence that he struck her three times with a switch about the size of her husband's finger. The size of the switch mattered because under the law as it stood in North Carolina and other places, a man could beat his wife as long as the switch he used was no bigger than his thumb—the so-called "rule of thumb." The trial court found the husband not guilty because the switch was smaller than his thumb.

She appealed to the North Carolina Supreme Court,

decade, the organization took for granted that women attending the convention would have a voice in the proceedings.

✦ ✦ ✦ ✦ ✦ ✦ ✦ ✦ ✦ ✦ ✦ ✦ ✦ ✦

Anthony and Stanton shocked the nation when they took up the cause of an impoverished immigrant woman named Hester Vaughn, who was convicted of murder and sentenced to die by hanging.

Betrayal

which also found the beating legal, but for a different reason. The North Carolina Supreme Court rejected the rule of thumb and said what mattered wasn't the size of the switch, but the extent of the injuries. Elizabeth's injuries were not serious, so her husband was fully entitled to give her "moderate correction."

"Every household must have a government of its own," the court said, "modeled to suit the temper, disposition, and condition" of its members. The court ended on a political note, remarking that just as the federal government had no business meddling in state affairs, courts had no business meddling in family affairs.

Hester had fallen in love with a man who abandoned her when she was expecting a baby. Hester found odd jobs working as a maid, and rented a dilapidated room. When she gave birth, she was alone without food or water in her room. Afterward she fell unconscious. It was hours before she could move from the room and call for help. By the time help arrived, the baby had died. Hester was brought to trial for murder. At her trial, she testified that the father of the baby was her former employer, who fired her and abandoned her when he discovered she was pregnant. Hester wept all through the trial and sentencing. According to the court, she "appeared still unable to comprehend her situation, and although the tears flowed freely, it appeared to be more the result of her desolate condition, abandoned as she was by everyone, than because of her probable death." When sentencing Hester to death, the judge said that the number of infants dying in such suspicious circumstances was on the rise, so some woman must be made an example of. He intended for that woman to be Hester.

Anthony and Stanton brought doctors to Hester in prison, and demanded that the governor pardon her. The governor refused, saying his hands were tied. The law was the law. Anthony and Stanton used their newspaper to ignite widespread support for Hester's plight, arguing that she'd been condemned on "inadequate proof" of murder, but plenty of proof that she had been betrayed and abandoned by the baby's father. "Men have made the law cunningly for their own protection," Stanton wrote. She suggested that the judge wanted to "satisfy the public lust for female blood" by "hanging a few women." Eventually, Anthony and Stanton secured a pardon for Hester and raised the money to send her back to her family in England.

Cartoon making fun of women's suffrage. A woman is smoking a cigar while a man holds a baby. They are voting for "Miss Hangman for Sheriff." The woman at the end of the line is a caricature of Susan B. Anthony. Currier & Ives, 1869.

✹ ✹ ✹ ✹ ✹ ✹ ✹ ✹ ✹ ✹ ✹ ✹ ✹ ✹ ✹

In February of 1869, Congress passed the Fifteenth Amendment as proposed. It was now time for the amendment to go to the states for ratification. The Equal Rights Association met to debate whether to endorse the amendment. Lucretia Mott, as president, presided. To Anthony's dismay, the men outnumbered the women, something she had tried to avoid by giving out tickets to women.

Not long into the meeting, Frederick Douglass "attempted to force the adoption" of a resolution, stating,

SUSAN B. ANTHONY

We gratefully welcome the pending Fifteenth Amendment prohibiting disfranchisement on account of race and earnestly solicit the State legislatures to pass it without delay.

Anthony jumped in and gave her standard objections. "The question of precedence has no place on an equal rights platform," she told him. "The only reason it ever forced itself here was because certain persons insisted that woman must stand back and wait until another class should be enfranchised."

Douglass insisted on framing the issue in terms of who should go first. He pit black men against white women, insisting that black men should go first and white women afterward. In doing so, he glossed over the fact that his suggestion meant black women would also go afterward.

"If Mr. Douglass had noticed who clapped for him," Anthony pointed out, "he would have seen they were all men."

Douglass persisted, saying, "I do not see how anyone can pretend there is the same urgency in giving the ballot to women as to the Negro. With us it is a matter of life and death . . . when women because they are women are hunted down . . . dragged from their homes and hung from lamp-posts, when their children are torn from their arms, and their brains dashed out upon the

Betrayal

pavement . . . then they will have an urgency to obtain the ballot equal to our own."

One of the women asked, "Is that not true about black women?"

"Yes, yes, yes," he conceded, "it is true of the black woman, but not because she is a woman, but because she is black."

Douglass assumed that if black men had the vote, they would take care of the black women. Anthony, seeing how white men often treated their wives, assumed the opposite. She asked him—outraged as he was with the way black men were treated—whether he would exchange his race *and* gender with Elizabeth Cady Stanton. Instead of responding, Douglass evoked laughter by asking whether women getting the right to vote would change anything "in respect to the nature of our sexes."

Anthony shot back that yes, much would be changed, the most important of which was "it will place her in a position in which she can earn her own bread." She then said, "If you are determined to extend the suffrage piece by piece, then give it first to women, to the most intelligent and capable portion at least, because in the present state of government it is intelligence, it is morality that is needed." The problem with the amendment, she said, was that it "wasn't equal rights. It puts two million more men in position of tyrants over two million women who had until now been the equal of the men by their sides." She repeated her main argument: "Neither [black men nor white women] has a claim to precedence upon an Equal Rights platform."

Anthony and Stanton were outvoted. The Equal Rights Association would endorse the Fifteenth Amendment as written. The next ruckus was caused when someone brought up the subject of divorce and called for a resolution that the group not try to tamper with the sanctity of marriage. There was some cheering in agreement.

Anthony again grabbed the floor and said, "This howl comes from the men who know that when women get their rights they will be able to live honestly and not be compelled to sell themselves for bread, either in or out of marriage."

✶ ✶ ✶ ✶ ✶ ✶ ✶ ✶ ✶ ✶ ✶ ✶ ✶ ✶ ✶

After the convention, Anthony, Stanton, and a group of disgruntled women representing nineteen different states gathered privately. They decided to break off and form a separate women's organization with the name National Woman Suffrage Association. They elected Elizabeth Cady Stanton as the first president, and laid out their goals and agenda. The

Betrayal

National Woman Suffrage Association would oppose the Fifteenth Amendment as written and address any issues that kept women in subservient positions and dependent upon men. Moreover, only women could be officers.

The larger, more conservative group, led by Lucy Stone, renamed themselves the American Woman Suffrage Association. The American Woman Suffrage Association backed the Fifteenth Amendment as written. Their goal was to campaign for the vote for women on a state-by-state basis. They limited themselves to the issue of suffrage, avoiding controversial issues that would offend the men. They allowed men to be officers. Henry Blackwell, Lucy Stone's husband, denounced the wider agenda of Anthony and Stanton, saying that "some insist" on raising such divisive issues as "temperance, marriage, race, dress, finance, labor, and capital," which in his view, damaged the women's movement. By limiting themselves to campaigning for women's vote on a state-by-state basis, the American Woman Suffrage Association was able to continue working closely with the Republican Party.

The National Woman Suffrage Association, in contrast, stung by the betrayal of the Republicans, declared themselves independent of all political parties. They would choose their candidates based on their stance on women's suffrage. Anthony made a firm decision going forward: She would keep racial issues and women's issues separate. Racial issues required working with and for men. Women as a group needed their own advocates.

The two women's groups would remain bitterly divided for more than twenty years. Anthony herself was pained over the split, and angry about how harshly her former allies criticized her for not backing an amendment giving black men the vote. One modern scholar, in explaining Anthony's position, said Anthony is best described as a "radical egalitarian"—one who holds all people absolutely equal and cannot abide any hierarchy. Anthony's refusal to support the Fifteenth Amendment because it did not include women came down to a matter of personality and character. Had she been able to support an amendment that lifted one group over another, she would not have been Susan B. Anthony.

✦ ✦ ✦ ✦ ✦ ✦ ✦ ✦ ✦ ✦ ✦ ✦ ✦ ✦ ✦

As with the Fourteenth Amendment, the Republicans were able to apply pressure to the states in the former Confederacy to get the Fifteenth Amendment ratified. On February 3, 1870, after being ratified by both Georgia and Iowa, the Fifteenth Amendment guaranteeing the vote for black men became part of the United States Constitution.

Illustration idealizing the changes that would come to blacks as a result of the Fifteenth Amendment. Temporarily, during Reconstruction, blacks enjoyed certain rights. After Reconstruction, it would be about one hundred years before blacks would begin to have equal access to education and voting booths because of strong resistance to black equality and devastating setbacks delivered by nineteenth- and early twentieth-century Supreme Court decisions. By E. Sachse & Co, Kahl, G. F. Schneider & Fuchs, 1870.

10

Let the World Wag

*"How do I keep so energetic?
By always being busy, by never having time
to think of myself, and never indulging
in any form of self-absorption."*
—Susan B. Anthony

The *Revolution* was failing. Part of the problem was that the rival women's organization, the American Woman Suffrage Association, launched their own newspaper, the *Woman's Journal*, which was more genteel and less radical, and took away many of the readers from the *Revolution*. As the *Revolution* lost subscribers, the paper faced bankruptcy. By 1870, Anthony and Stanton had to shut it down completely. Anthony personally absorbed the debt, which took her years to pay off from her earnings as a lecturer.

Let the World Wag

In 1871, Anthony and Stanton decided to take their message to the women of the western states and territories with a tour of California, Colorado, Wyoming, Utah, Nevada, and then Oregon and Washington. They traveled by train, enjoying the spectacular scenery and the quiet time together. When they arrived in San Francisco, they received a warm welcome. The local newspapers had announced their visit, so when they reached the Grand Hotel, where they were staying, they found gifts of fruit, flowers, and invitations.

The city was then gripped by a sensational murder case. An unmarried woman with a scandalous reputation, Laura Fair, had been found guilty of murdering a man who had lied to her and betrayed her. The man she killed was one of the city's most prominent lawyers. What happened was this: He declared he was in love with her and promised to marry her. After she fell in love and agreed to marry him, she discovered that he was already married. Enraged, she tracked him down

Laura Fair, originally published in the *San Francisco Chronicle*, 1870–1871

and shot him. She was found guilty of murder and sentenced to death. Shortly after arriving in San Francisco, Anthony and Stanton went to visit her in jail.

That evening, the lecture hall was packed. Anthony took the stage and gave a speech called "The Power of the Ballot" in which she debunked the argument that women didn't need to vote because their husbands, brothers, and adult sons protected them. She pointed to the fact that thirteen hundred babies had been left in baskets at the New York foundling hospital as proof that at least thirteen hundred women in New York were not protected by men.

All went well until she said, "If all the men protected all the women, you would have no Laura Fair in jail tonight." The hall erupted. From all corners came hissing—a sound she was well accustomed to from the days she lectured on abolition and black equality. She waited for silence, then repeated the offending sentence and continued with her speech. Now a scattering of cheers were mixed in with the storm of hisses. People tried to boo her from the stage, but she stood firm, encouraged by those who were cheering. She closed by saying, "I declare to you that woman must not depend upon the protection of a man, but must be taught to protect herself, and there I take my stand."

Let the World Wag

The next morning, every local paper came out against her. One newspaper accused her of saying she approved of the murder. The story was picked up by national papers, most of which denounced her as well. The outcry was so fierce that her other talks and appearances in San Francisco were canceled. In her own words, she had "never before got such a raking." Her sister Mary wrote encouraging letters. "It is scandalous the way the newspapers talk about you," she wrote, "but stick to what you feel is right and let the world wag."

During the fury over Anthony's Laura Fair comments, Stanton learned that her mother had fallen ill. Stanton, who was less comfortable than Anthony in facing hostile crowds, returned home to care for her mother. Anthony completed the tour of the West alone. Everywhere she went, people came to hear her speak—and pay the price of admission. Some people came for the sole purpose of hissing and booing. Others came because they admired her audacity in speaking about a woman's need for independence.

By this time, Anthony was considered a national celebrity, so the press followed her, and whenever she spoke, her words were reported in the newspapers. One newspaper dismissed her as a "strident spinster." According to another: "Ask nine men out of ten to give you their idea of Miss Anthony, and they will describe to you a woman unsexed—a witch personified." This same reporter went on to declare that Anthony's heart was drained of everything "but hate of men." Another newspaper accused her of plotting to corrupt wives and daughters. The editor of Oregon City's *Weekly Enterprise* repeated the popular theory that her anger came from her misfortune in never marrying. "We could not help thinking what a fine looking and useful woman she would have been had she got married years ago," said the editor. "We wish she had been more fortunate in her younger days."

Women were often just as harsh. For example, one woman who met Anthony in Oregon wrote, "I could never see how it was that an Old Maid who neglected to fill the office in society for which God

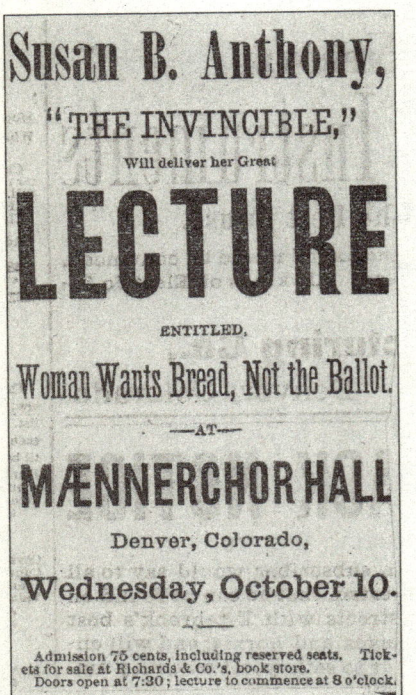

Handbill advertising Anthony's lecture debunking the popular notion that "a woman wants nothing but a home with her daily needs supplied"

in his providence had wisely created her, should essay [*sic*] to lecture married women."

When Anthony's critics pointed out that the large numbers of women didn't *want* to vote, she responded by saying, "If women do not desire the right to vote, it is evidence of the depth to which they have been degraded by its deprivation."

✱ ✱ ✱ ✱ ✱ ✱ ✱ ✱ ✱ ✱ ✱ ✱ ✱ ✱ ✱

A charismatic and ambitious newcomer to the women's movement, Victoria Woodhull, got the idea to ask the House of Representatives for clarity on the meaning of the Fourteenth Amendment. Woodhull wanted a public statement from Congress that in devising the amendment, they had not intended to leave women out. Anthony went with Woodhull when she made her presentation to Congress. When Woodhull finished

Victoria Woodhull appeared with Anthony in front of the House of Representatives. She was also the first woman to run for president in 1872, although her candidacy gained no traction. Date and photographer unknown.

speaking, Anthony turned to those congressmen who had worked with her on behalf of black rights and pleaded with them to offer a declaratory act that women were included in the phrase "all persons."

One month after the women put their plea before Congress, Senator John A. Bingham, the author of the amendment's crucial language, announced that, in fact, he had intended for women *not* to be included.

Some of the "ablest constitutional lawyers in the country" put forward another option for the women. These constitutional experts believed that the women had a strong legal argument under the plain language theory of constitutional interpretation, which said that when a word in a statute is clear and unambiguous, courts must honor the plain meaning of the word, regardless of what was intended. The plain language approach was the preferred one, these scholars argued, because it prevented courts from imposing their own meanings onto words and taking sides in a political debate. The plain language theory in this case was a simple one: The Fourteenth Amendment used the term "persons," and women were persons. Therefore, despite what Bingham said, women were included. Surely voting was one of the "privileges and immunities" guaranteed to all citizens. Thus women were guaranteed the right to vote under the Fourteenth Amendment.

Women decided to test the theory by registering to vote. Most were turned way. Anthony wanted to try to register, but the local laws in Rochester required a person to be in residence for thirty days prior to the election to be eligible, and she was rarely at home for that long. The first election in which she met the thirty-day residency requirement was in November 1872. On November 1, 1872, she was at home in Rochester with her mother and sister Mary when she opened the newspaper and read: "Now register! Today and tomorrow are the only remaining opportunities!"

Anthony rounded up her three sisters—Guelma, Mary, and Hannah—and marched them all to the Rochester barbershop where three registrars were signing up voters. Anthony instructed the men to register them. The men, nervous, hesitated. So Anthony took out a copy of the Constitution and read the part where all persons were entitled to equal protection of the laws and the privileges and immunities of citizenship. The men called their supervisor and they talked among themselves about what to do. When Anthony promised to personally pay their fines should they get into trouble, they relented. By the end of the day, fifteen women had registered in that precinct. By the following day, fifty women had registered in various precincts all over the state.

Anthony called on several lawyers to ask for advice about what to do on election day, but each refused to represent her. At last, she found a lawyer willing to advise her, Henry R. Selden, formerly a judge on the court of appeals. He considered her arguments, told her that both he and his brother, who was also a lawyer, believed that women did indeed have a right to vote under the Fourteenth Amendment. He promised to represent her, and protect her to the best of his ability.

Early on election day, November 5, 1872, Anthony, her sisters, and a few other women showed up to vote. When poll workers hesitated, she promised to take full responsibility should anyone get into trouble. The poll workers allowed the women to vote. Anthony cast her ballot for Republican candidate Ulysses S. Grant because he promised that women's demands would be given a respectful hearing.

After returning home, she wrote to Stanton, "Well, I have been and gone and done it, positively voted this morning at 7 o'clock, and swore my vote in at that. Not a jeer, not a rude word, not a disrespectful look has met one woman . . . I hope you voted, too."

Two weeks after the election, Anthony was at home when

Let the World Wag

Deputy United States Marshal E. J. Keeney knocked on the door and explained that he was there to arrest her. He brought her to the local commissioner, who ordered her and the other women who had voted to return with their lawyers for a preliminary hearing. At the preliminary hearing, the judge set bail for each woman at five hundred dollars. Anthony had no intention of paying the bail. She preferred to sit in prison to draw attention to her case, but unbeknownst to her, her lawyer paid her bail for her. He said he couldn't stand to think of a lady in prison.

Anthony was indicted by a grand jury. The grand jury easily determined that of the women who had voted that day, she was the leader and instigator. She was therefore the only woman of the fifteen ordered to stand trial. The others were indicted, but their cases were dismissed in exchange for a promise that they would not try to vote again.

While out on bail, Anthony talked openly about the details of her arrest. She insisted that her rights as a citizen included the right to vote, and she lectured on the question "Is it a crime for a United States citizen to vote?" Fellow suffragist Frances Gage announced that the United States was on trial, not Susan B. Anthony. Some newspapers, like the *Rochester Union*, declared that Anthony was a "corruptionist" and accused her

★ ★ ★ ★ ★ SUSAN B. ANTHONY ★ ★ ★ ★ ★

Political cartoon entitled "The Woman Who Dared" (to vote), Thomas Wust, artist, June 15, 1873

Let the World Wag

of attempting to use the courts to stage the "enactment of a comedy." Other newspapers talked of her courage and her quest for justice and equality.

On the grounds that she had tainted the jury pool by talking about her case, her trial was moved to another district. For one reason after another, her trial was delayed until June 17, 1873. The trial was held in the village of Canandaigua, New York. In the crowded courtroom were many prominent politicians, including former president Millard Fillmore. The evidence against her was simply that she was a woman and she had voted. She wanted to testify in her own defense, but the judge ruled that as a woman, she was incompetent to testify in court. He allowed her lawyer to present her defense.

The judge listened to her lawyer's constitutional arguments. When her lawyer finished talking, the judge took a paper from his pocket and read his decision—proving to an indignant Anthony that he had already decided the outcome before even showing up for the trial. His conclusion was that the Fourteenth Amendment did not grant Anthony the right to vote. On that basis, he refused to allow the jury to deliberate, instead directing them to find her guilty. Later Anthony called the trial an "outrage."

After pronouncing Anthony guilty, the judge turned to her

and asked if she had anything to say before her sentence was passed.

All eyes were on her. What followed was a moment of "sublime silence," as she later called it. Then she said, "Yes, Your Honor, I have many things to say. My every right, constitutional, civil, political and judicial have been tramped upon. I have not only had no jury of my peers, but I have had no jury at all."

"Sit down," the judge ordered. "I cannot allow you to argue the question."

"I shall not sit down . . . I will not lose my only chance to speak."

"You have been tried, Miss Anthony, by the forms of law, and my decision has been rendered by law."

"Yes, but laws made by men, under a government of men, interpreted by men, for the benefit of men." She then went on to explain that just as people of conscience ignored laws that were unjust to slaves, she intended to defy laws unjust to women.

When at last she sat down, the court passed sentence, ordering her to pay a fine of one hundred dollars and the costs of prosecution. When she said she had no money, but in fact, was in debt, the judge surprised her by saying he would not imprison her for not paying the fine. Later she understood why. If she refused to pay the fine, and the court refused to enforce the fine, she would be unable to appeal to a higher court. She never paid the fine, and the court never did anything about it.

After her trial, in her speeches, she reminded people of her status:

> *My friends, I stand before you tonight a convicted criminal [a burst of applause] . . . for what? For asserting my right to representative government, based upon the one idea of the right of every person governed to participate in that government.*

✻ ✻ ✻ ✻ ✻ ✻ ✻ ✻ ✻ ✻ ✻ ✻ ✻ ✻ ✻

Not long after Anthony's trial, her older sister, Guelma, fell ill with tuberculosis. Guelma, who was now fifty-five years old, was sick for many months, cared for by her sisters, her mother, and her married daughter. Her youngest sister, Mary, was with her when she died, on the morning of November 6, 1873. Anthony was beside herself with grief over the loss of her "dear elder sister, only seventeen months my senior . . . so close we were cradled together." One month later, Anthony and her sisters, still in the throes of grief, marked their mother's eightieth birthday.

★ ★ ★ ★ ★ ★ SUSAN B. ANTHONY ★ ★ ★ ★ ★ ★

★ ★ ★ ★ ★ ★ ★ ★ ★ ★ ★ ★ ★ ★ ★

Another member of the National Woman Suffrage Association, Virginia Minor, was able to take her voting rights case all the way to the United States Supreme Court. The facts of Minor's case were straightforward. When she tried to register to vote in St. Louis, the officials refused to allow her to register, so she brought a lawsuit alleging that she had been denied the privileges and immunities of citizenship guaranteed by the Fourteenth Amendment.

Virginia Minor as she appeared in 1850.
John Chester Buttre, photographer;
J. A. Scholtern, engraver

The Supreme Court ruled against her and delivered a devastating setback to the women's movement. The court held that the privileges and immunities of citizenship were not defined by the United States Constitution, so individual states could define privileges and immunities any way they wanted to. The court held that Missouri's law allowing only men to vote did not violate the Constitution because Missouri could decide for itself whether the privileges and immunities clause included the right to vote.

Let the World Wag

The ruling was part of a pattern the Supreme Court had adopted of taking the teeth out of the Fourteenth Amendment and returning power to the states. Just as the Supreme Court interpreted the Fourteenth Amendment against women's rights, so too the court interpreted the amendment against black freedom, finding reasons to conclude that many of the black codes enacted in the South did not violate the "equal protection" clause of the Fourteenth Amendment.

The very next year, the Supreme Court ruled against a woman named Myra Bradwell. She claimed that Illinois denied her rights under the Fourteenth Amendment when it refused to allow her a license to practice law because she was a woman. This time the court based its ruling on the intent of the drafters, saying the purpose of the Fourteenth Amendment was to offer freedom to former slaves, not equal rights to women. Therefore, Illinois was within its rights to refuse Bradwell permission to practice law. The Supreme Court added that women should not be practicing law anyway because

> *The natural and proper timidity and delicacy which belongs to the female sex evidently unfits it for many of the occupations of civil life. The constitution of the family*

organization, which is founded in the divine ordinance as well as in the nature of things, indicates the domestic sphere as that which properly belongs to the domain and function of womanhood.

One concurring Justice gave his oft quoted conclusion:

The paramount destiny and mission of woman are to fulfill the noble and benign offices of wife and mother. This is the law of the Creator. And the rules of civil society must be adapted to the general constitution of things, and cannot be based upon exceptional cases.

Women in search of legal equality, thus, had no hope of finding it in the federal courts. Elizabeth Cady Stanton, growing tired of men making the laws and issuing rulings that women must obey, likened the situation to "clowns" making "laws for queens."

✶ ✶ ✶ ✶ ✶ ✶ ✶ ✶ ✶ ✶ ✶ ✶ ✶ ✶ ✶

As the nation's hundredth birthday approached, officials and politicians planned July Fourth celebrations across the country, with a grand celebration in Philadelphia, the birthplace of the United States. Women's groups discussed how they would protest the fact that they were still not included in "we the people." Some women wanted to march solemnly, as in a funeral, carrying signs that said "Taxation without representation is tyranny."

Anthony, Stanton, and a few other members of the National Woman Suffrage Association devised their own plan. Upon learning that the Declaration of Independence would be read from the stage during the Philadelphia celebration, they drafted the Declaration of Rights of the Women of the United States. The Declaration began on a solemn note:

> *While the Nation is buoyant with patriotism, and all hearts are attuned to praise, it is with sorrow we come to strike one discordant note, on this hundredth anniversary of our country's birth.*

And followed with a statement of resentment:

> *Yet we cannot forget, even in this glad hour, that while men of every race and clime, and condition, have been invested with the full rights of citizenship under our hospitable flag, all women still suffer the degradation of disenfranchisement.*

The four-page document went on to demand for women each of the rights possessed by men. They printed thousands of copies. Anthony asked General Joseph R. Hawley, president of the United States Centennial Commission, for permission for a woman to speak on the stage. He denied the request. She then asked for seats for fifty officers of the National Woman Suffrage Association. He denied that, also. So she obtained a press pass through her brother's newspaper. Then, shortly before the celebration, the commissioner sent the women six tickets for admission. Stanton and Lucretia Mott, insulted, refused to attend. But "others more brave and determined . . . decided to take the risk of public insult in order to present the woman's declaration and thus make it a historical document." In other words, Anthony decided to crash the stage.

Anthony positioned herself and a few co-conspirators close to the stage. The ceremony opened when Richard Henry Lee, a statesman from Virginia, read the Declaration of Independence aloud. When Lee finished reading, Anthony and her associates rose from their seats and marched to the platform. The men, startled, didn't stop them. Standing on the stage was United States vice president Thomas W. Ferry. Anthony handed Ferry a rolled-up copy of the Declaration of Women. His "face paled, as bowing low, he received the declaration."

Richard Henry Lee reading the original document of the Declaration of Independence at the centennial celebration in Philadelphia, 1876

General Joseph R. Hawley banged a gavel and shouted, "Order! Order!" What followed was pandemonium as Anthony and her associates handed copies to anyone who reached for one. Some men climbed over chairs to get a copy. Anthony and her four co-conspirators continued handing out copies to people as they marched out of the hall.

11
A New Generation

"We shall someday [have our amendment]—everybody will think it was always so, just exactly as many young people think that all the privileges, all the freedom, all the enjoyments which woman now possesses always were hers. They have no idea of how every single inch of ground that she stands upon today has been gained by the hard work of some little handful of women of the past."

—*Susan B. Anthony*

Anthony, Stanton, and one of their fellow reformers, Matilda Joslyn Gage, decided to undertake a major writing project: a history of the struggle for women's rights in America. "Men have been faithful in noting every heroic act of their half of the race," Anthony explained. It was now the duty of women "to make for future generations a record of the heroic deeds of the other half."

Anthony handled the business end of the project. Stanton did most of the writing and editing. Gathering information for

A New Generation

the book required going back over decades of activism, sifting through boxes of newspaper articles and magazine clippings. At times Anthony found the strain of wading through articles and letters too painful to bear. "It makes me sad and tired," she wrote, "to read them over, to see the terrible strain I was under every minute then, have been since, am now and shall be for the rest of my life."

During the early stages of research and writing the *History of Woman Suffrage*, Anthony's sister Hannah fell ill with a mysterious illness. The family decided to send her to Kansas in the hopes that she might recover there—a decision Anthony firmly disagreed with. When the doctors pronounced Hannah's condition hopeless, Anthony headed west to be with her sister. She arrived in Leavenworth on April 20, 1877, and scarcely left her sister's side during the final weeks of her illness. Hannah died on May 12, 1877.

✷ ✷ ✷ ✷ ✷ ✷ ✷ ✷ ✷ ✷ ✷ ✷ ✷ ✷ ✷

On January 10, 1878, Senator Aaron Sargent presented to Congress a Sixteenth Amendment guaranteeing women the right to vote. Anthony and Stanton testified before the Senate Committee on Privileges and Elections in support of the amendment. Anthony later said that the senators on the committee—most of whom were many years younger than she was—treated her with outright contempt. One senator yawned and gazed at the ceiling. Another sharpened his pencil. "It was difficult," she said. "I restrained the impulse . . . to hurl my manuscript at his head." The amendment went nowhere.

Each year for the remainder of her life, Anthony and others returned to Congress and reintroduced the amendment. Each year they were dismissed and rejected.

✦ ✦ ✦ ✦ ✦ ✦ ✦ ✦ ✦ ✦ ✦ ✦ ✦ ✦ ✦

In early 1880, Lucy Read Anthony, approaching the age of eighty-seven, became ill. Anthony limited her lectures to those near Rochester so she could remain close to her mother. Lucy died in April, leaving Anthony and her sister Mary alone in the Rochester house. Some years earlier, Mary had purchased the house from her mother, so the two sisters were secure in their home. Mary kept the house while Anthony resumed her work, traveling, lecturing, inspiring, and organizing women in each state.

The first volume of *History of Woman Suffrage* was published

A New Generation

in 1881, and recounted women's earliest attempts to achieve equality with men. The second volume, published in 1885, covered the movement during the years of the Civil War and immediately after. Four additional volumes would follow over the next seven years.

At about this time, Anthony became interested in women's suffrage movements in Europe. She, Stanton, and several others made plans for an International Council of Women. The idea was to form a council of women in each country to work for suffrage for women everywhere. The organization was founded in 1888, and held its first conference.

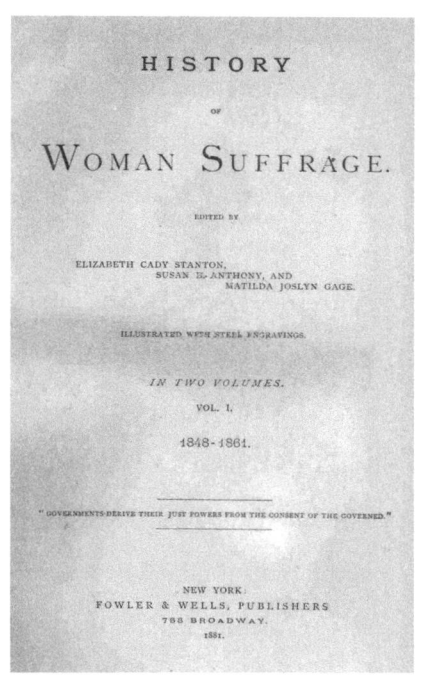

Title page of *History of Woman Suffrage*

In the course of her international work, Anthony made several trips to Europe. During one trip to England, Queen Victoria invited a group of suffragists, including Anthony, to tea at Windsor Castle. Anthony was not impressed with the Queen

★★★★★★ SUSAN B. ANTHONY ★★★★★★

of England. As a radical egalitarian, she viewed a queen as no more elevated than any other person. Moreover, Anthony scoffed that "in all matters connected with women she has been very conservative." With the same Quaker defiance for the British social order that caused her ancestors to have to flee England, Anthony could never seem to get the titles right, and kept saying "Mr." and "Mrs." instead of "your lordship" and "your ladyship."

Anthony may not have thought much of the queen, but Victoria's subjects were enamored with Anthony. One headline in London read "Miss Anthony the London Sensation." The article noted that, unlike the "loud-voiced strident" suffragists London was accustomed to, "Miss Anthony's slim figure, severe face, and smoothly banded hair was an innovation."

In Italy, Anthony shocked those listening to her, including a few members of the Italian aristocracy, when she gazed at a magnificent palace and remarked that it would make a marvelous orphanage and could probably house up to seven hundred homeless children.

While in Germany, she accidentally got herself into a bit of trouble. Thinking nothing of it, she mailed letters in the usual envelopes she used, which had National Woman Suffrage Association mottos printed on them: "Taxation Without

A New Generation

Representation is Tyranny," and "No just government can be formed without the consent of the governed." It didn't occur to her that Germany was a monarchy, and the government might not appreciate such notions. Sure enough, a German government official came to visit, handed back the letters, and told her they would not be allowed through the German postage system. She put the letters into plain envelopes so she could mail them. Stanton, learning of the incident, remarked that "It is well for us that she did not experiment in Russia [where critics of the government were dealt with much more harshly] or we should now be mourning her loss as an exile in Siberia."

✦ ✦ ✦ ✦ ✦ ✦ ✦ ✦ ✦ ✦ ✦ ✦ ✦ ✦ ✦

The younger women coming into the women's movement had no firsthand memories of how the two women's groups—the National Woman Suffrage Association and the American Woman Suffrage Association—came to be divided. At any rate, the differences between the two groups were fading. Anthony was becoming more focused on women's suffrage, which brought her more in line with the American Woman Suffrage Association. While Stanton continued reeling off opinions that set people on edge, some of Stanton and Anthony's ideas, including their ideas on divorce, which once seemed so radical, were no longer shocking. By that time, courts were routinely allowing women to petition for divorce based upon proof that their husbands were beating them.

Negotiations for a reunion of the two groups began in about 1887. While the younger women were eager for a union, the elders—still holding their grudges—resisted. At last, in 1890 in Washington, D.C., the two groups combined a celebration of Anthony's seventieth birthday with final meetings to unite the two groups. The new, united organization adopted the name of the National American Woman Suffrage Association.

Lucy Stone, who was still the nominal head of the more conservative group, was feeling weak and unwell, so she withdrew her name from consideration as the first president. The majority of others preferred Anthony to Stanton, but Anthony said she wanted Stanton to be president, so Stanton was elected. Lucy Stone agreed to chair the executive committee and Anthony agreed to serve as vice president at large. The group would focus primarily on gaining votes for women in individual states while working to secure a constitutional amendment guaranteeing women the right to vote.

One of the first goals of the National American Woman

A New Generation

Suffrage Association was voting rights in Colorado—a state in which victory seemed likely. The suffragist leader in Colorado, Carrie Chapman Catt, was a young woman in her early thirties and a protégé of Anthony. Catt had attended college in Iowa, and after graduating, joined the women's suffrage movement there. She became known as one of the best organizers in Iowa, and traveled to Washington, D.C., to attend the 1890 conference in which the American Woman Suffrage Association and National Woman Suffrage Association merged. Anthony was impressed with Catt's energy, dedication, and talent as a speaker, and helped her move up in the organization. When the women in Colorado wanted to campaign for suffrage in the state, they asked Anthony for help. Anthony sent Catt. In 1893, as a result of Catt's efforts, Colorado granted women the right to vote.

When they were territories, Utah and Wyoming had allowed women to vote. When

Carrie Chapman Catt led the suffrage movement in Colorado and later served as chairperson of the National American Woman Suffrage Association between 1895 and 1900. Portrait Studio of Theodore C. Marceau, 1896.

they entered statehood, Wyoming in 1890 and Utah in 1896, they joined as states in which women could vote. Idaho voted to enfranchise women in 1896, bringing the number of states allowing women to vote up to four. Success tended to come in the West, where the establishment was a little less set, and customs a little less entrenched. Because of the shortage of men in the West, women often did work typically thought of as men's work. Moreover, western men wanted to make their states attractive to female settlers from the East. It was therefore easier to persuade western men to share political power with women.

Meanwhile, New Zealand became the first country to allow women to vote, followed by Australia in 1902. Thus internationally, as in the United States, the newer more sparsely populated communities were the first to embrace women's suffrage.

★ ★ ★ ★ ★ ★ ★ ★ ★ ★ ★ ★ ★ ★ ★

During the second half of the nineteenth century, more and more women's colleges were springing up, and more of the established colleges were opening their doors to women. The women's colleges became natural centers for young

A New Generation

activists. Young women in growing numbers questioned the laws that kept them from having a voice in government and prevented them from entering professions like law, medicine, science, and politics. One young woman after another read the Fourteenth Amendment, believed that she was a person and therefore the amendment included her, and added her voice to the clamor for women's rights.

Other long-fought-for changes were also occurring. Most states now allowed married women to own property, if they brought the property with them into the marriage, and allowed them to control their own earnings, if they drew a salary.

Along with these changes, there arose a backlash in the form of a strong anti–women's rights movement, led by conservative women who argued, among other things, that upsetting the separate spheres for women would create unrest in America and undermine any hope for peace and prosperity. They believed that a woman's power rested in the home. They also insisted that a woman's power in the home was the equivalent to a man's power in the public sphere. Because women were essentially nurturers, the argument went, they should not involve themselves in politics. Anthony reminded the female anti-suffragists that "but for the suffrage movement they would not have had the privilege of

Elizabeth Cady Stanton and Susan B. Anthony, date and photographer unknown

A New Generation

coming before men in public to criticize and ask that we not be given the things we pray for."

✶ ✶ ✶ ✶ ✶ ✶ ✶ ✶ ✶ ✶ ✶ ✶ ✶ ✶ ✶

Stanton was five years older than Anthony. At eighty, she was ready to slow down, but Anthony urged her to keep going. Anthony worried that if they stopped working, the women's movement would lose momentum. Stanton disagreed. "I tried to assure her that the earth would turn on its axis after she & I ascended to Abraham's bosom."

Mary Anthony, photographed by John Howe Kent, 1897

Once, when talking about Anthony, Stanton quoted Ralph Waldo Emerson, saying that "It is better to be a thorn in the side of your friend than his echo." Anthony freely admitted that she had often been a thorn in her friend's side, often disagreeing with her, always prodding her on. In fact, Stanton, with her tendency toward hyperbole, once said that Anthony kept her going "at the point of the bayonet." Instead of graciously allowing Stanton to

SUSAN B. ANTHONY

slow down as she entered her eighties, Anthony got the idea for Stanton, now a widow, to move into a spare room in her Rochester home so that they could be more productive. Stanton's children put their foot down and said no.

* * * * * * * * * * * * * * *

Ida Husted Harper, approximately 1900, Bain News Service, publisher

In 1897, Anthony selected Ida Husted Harper, a journalist and suffragist, to write her official biography. Harper moved into the Anthony home in Rochester to write the book so that she could easily consult with Anthony and so she would have easy access to all of Anthony's papers, which took up two full rooms. Once again, Anthony found herself going through letters, scrapbooks, and diaries. She was so determined for every detail to be recorded accurately that she asked some people to return the letters she had written them. The first two volumes were published in 1898 and 1899. Meanwhile, Anthony kept up her travel and touring schedule.

A New Generation

Anthony, who had never indulged much in games or frivolity, attended her first football game in 1898 in Chicago. From her seat near the fifty-yard line, she asked her companions, "Why don't they kick the ball?" She enjoyed the afternoon. She didn't think much of football, though. "There's no game to it," she reported later. "At least I can't see any. They take the ball and then fall down in heaps. It's ridiculous. The boys who play don't look like human beings at all. At first I thought they resembled apes, but after they got to plowing about in the mud they reminded me more of the seals I saw in the Pacific when last in California." In response to mothers worrying that their sons would be hurt, she said, "I failed to see anyone hurt . . . It's silly, not brutal."

She did, however, approve of the new bicycle craze—and she particularly enjoyed seeing women on bicycles. In her opinion, bicycles had done "a great deal to emancipate women. I stand and rejoice every time I see a woman ride by on a wheel. It gives her a feeling of freedom, self-reliance, and independence . . . The bicycle also teaches practical dress reform, gives women fresh air and exercise, and makes them equal with men." She even imagined how the bicycle might help bring about women's suffrage. "When bicyclists want a bit of special legislation, such as side-paths and laws to protect them, or to compel railroads to

"Miss Bicycle," by Boussod, Valadon & Co., 1884. Women participated in the bicycle craze of the late 1800s.

A New Generation

check them as baggage, the women are likely to be made to see that their petitions would be more respected by law-makers if they had votes."

Meanwhile, Anthony was "continually exploring new fields for missionary labors." She established a press bureau to feed articles on women's rights to the mainstream press. She also worked on getting the University of Rochester to admit women. Nearby Cornell and Syracuse had opened their doors to women, but the University of Rochester resisted. The university officials listened to the pleas from the women, but insisted that they needed additional funds for women's facilities. So Anthony raised the money herself, and then appeared before the board of directors and made her plea. That evening, she wrote in her diary: "They let the girls in—said there was no alternative."

✶ ✶ ✶ ✶ ✶ ✶ ✶ ✶ ✶ ✶ ✶ ✶ ✶ ✶ ✶

At the age of eighty, Anthony suffered two minor strokes. Her doctors advised her to slow her pace, but she refused, saying, "I feel it would be just as well if I reached the end on cars." At the 1900 meeting of the National American Woman Suffrage Association, however, she resigned her leadership position. She assured the assembly of much younger women that "I am not retiring now because I feel unable, mentally or physically, to do the necessary work, but because I want to see . . . you all at work while I am alive, so I can scold you if you do not do it well." The group insisted that Anthony retain the title of honorary president.

She tried to keep to her same schedule, but the following year she acknowledged that she was no longer able to do as much. "I suppose at eighty-one," she wrote to a friend, "we must naturally begin to feel a change come over us." The frustrating part was that the grand prize—a constitutional amendment guaranteeing women the right to vote—still seemed out of reach. "Oh, if I could but live another century," she told an interviewer, "and see the fruition of all the work for women!" She cultivated close relationships with the younger women of the organization, who she would have to trust to carry on with the work. She called them her nieces, and they called her "Aunt Susan."

In October of 1902, Anthony wrote Stanton a letter, reflecting back on their fifty years of friendship and partnership:

We little dreamed when we began this contest, optimistic with the hope and buoyancy of youth, that half a century later we would be compelled to leave the finish of the battle

A New Generation

to another generation of women. But our hearts are filled with joy to know that they enter upon this task equipped with a college education, with business experience, with the fully admitted right to speak in public—all of which were denied to women fifty years ago.

Later that month, on October 26, 1902, a Western Union messenger knocked on the door of Anthony's home in Rochester. It was a message from one of Stanton's daughters telling Anthony that "Mother passed away today." Anthony sank into a chair and gazed at Stanton's portrait on the wall. The next day, she was on a train to New York City for the funeral. Stanton had left instructions. At the head of her casket, she wanted the table on which, in 1848, she had written the Declaration of Sentiments that launched the women's movement. When the table was moved into place, someone put on top a framed portrait of Susan B. Anthony.

✯ ✯ ✯ ✯ ✯ ✯ ✯ ✯ ✯ ✯ ✯ ✯ ✯ ✯ ✯

In 1904, Anthony attended the International Council of Women in Berlin. She remarked that seeing the spread of the women's movement across the globe was "the climax of my career." That same year, her brother Daniel died. She had now

Anthony (*circled*) seated at the International Council of Women in Berlin, 1904

outlived all of her siblings except the youngest, Mary, with whom she still lived in their Rochester home. Anthony didn't know until Daniel's will was read aloud that after taking care of his own wife, he left an annuity to be paid to both of his unmarried sisters for the remainder of their lives.

Anthony was then eighty-four years old. "The face is wrinkled now," one reporter wrote. "Her hair, in its demure Quaker coil, is almost as abundant as ever, but silver-white . . . She is a picaresque as well as impressive old lady, for she is always gowned in black satin, with a good bit of white at the throat . . . She is always on the alert, either to meet an argument, for which purposely she carries a whole army of intellectual weapons, or

A New Generation

to see a joke, in which she is far quicker than most women, or to make one, at which she is also adroit. She is persistently amiable, and absolutely tireless."

In 1905, Anthony met with President Theodore Roosevelt in Washington, D.C., about submitting a suffrage amendment to Congress. The president was clearly not interested. She asked him if he would mention women's suffrage in his speech. He told her he would recognize women as "wives, as mothers, as wage earners, but never with any reference to political rights." Next she tried a different approach. She told him that if, before he left the presidential chair, he would see to an amendment guaranteeing women the vote, he would take his "place in history with Lincoln, the Great Emancipator." He gave her no response.

That same year, former president Grover Cleveland remarked that women's clubs were harmful because they challenged the very nature of motherhood and wifehood, and thus posed a danger to society. He quoted the maxim that the hand that rocks the cradle rules the world. When a Rochester newspaper reporter came to Anthony and asked her for her response, she let loose a tirade. "Ridiculous!" she said. "Why isn't the woman herself the best judge of what woman's sphere should be? The men have been trying to tell us for years." In response to

★★★★★★ SUSAN B. ANTHONY ★★★★★★

Cleveland's comment about how the hand that rocks the cradle rules the world, she said, "That would be all right if you could keep the boys in the cradle always." The *Minneapolis Journal* responded with a cartoon showing Susan B. Anthony chasing Cleveland with an umbrella while Uncle Sam laughs in the background.

The majority of men in power had not changed their attitudes toward women's suffrage—but much of the public had. The same year Anthony met with President Roosevelt, she took a trip west and spoke at a reception at the Lewis and Clark Exposition in Oregon on June 30, 1905, which had been designated "Women's Day." While standing on the stage, Anthony was deluged by tossed bouquets of flowers. "This is rather different from the receptions I used to get fifty years ago," she told her audience. "They threw things at me then—but they were not roses."

Anthony chasing Cleveland, who is carrying a book that says, "What I know about women's clubs." Cartoon created by Charles Lewis Bartholomew, 1905.

★ ★ ★ ★ ★ ★ ★ ★

A New Generation

On Anthony's eighty-sixth birthday, her supporters and friends insisted on holding a birthday celebration for her in Washington, D.C. She agreed, and traveled by train to the capital.

Her birthday celebration was held at the Church of Our Father at Thirteenth and L Streets. She sat in a comfortable chair on the stage and listened to the accolades. Among those who sent birthday wishes were President Theodore Roosevelt, whose letter was read aloud from the podium. He sent his "hearty good wishes for the continuation of her useful and honorable life." Anthony was not impressed. She stood up and, with every bit of her youthful fire, said, "I wish men would do something besides extend congratulations . . . I would rather have President Roosevelt say one nice word to Congress in favor of amending the Constitution to give women the suffrage than to praise me endlessly!"

Two days later, she returned home to Rochester. She felt so weak that she had trouble climbing the stairs. At last she made it to her room and her bed. She'd come down with pneumonia. It was to be her final illness. As she lay dying, one of the women who sat with her was Anna Shaw, a member of the younger generation of women's rights leaders. Anthony, slipping from consciousness,

SUSAN B. ANTHONY

Reverend Anna Shaw, 1922, photographer unknown

began to utter the names of the women in her life, the women's rights activists, some who were still at work, some who had abandoned the cause, and others who neither Anna nor Mary had ever heard of. Anthony regained consciousness and rested her cheek on Anna's hand. "They are still passing before me—face after face, hundreds and hundreds of them," she said. "I know how hard they have worked. I know the sacrifices they have made."

Years earlier, on a magnificent summer day during a reunion in Anthony's birthplace in Adams, Massachusetts, someone remarked that the line of horse-drawn carriages looked like a funeral. "When it is a funeral," Anthony had said, "remember that I want there to be no tears. Pass on, and go on with the work."

12
Afterward

The mayor of Rochester ordered the flags at half-mast. Twelve women dressed in white kept a vigil around Anthony's casket while ten thousand mourners passed by to pay their final respects. Her sister Mary sat nearby, clutching a handkerchief but bravely holding back the tears. Anthony was dressed in her customary black. On her collar was an American flag pin given to her by the women of Utah. The pin had only four stars, tiny diamonds, representing the four states that allowed women to vote.

SUSAN B. ANTHONY

Twenty-five hundred people attended the funeral, while hundreds more stood outside. The honor bearers were women from the University of Rochester, dressed in black and carrying flowers.

The first speaker was abolitionist William Lloyd Garrison Jr., son of the man with whom Anthony had worked on behalf of black freedom, and with whom she had quarreled over the Fifteenth Amendment. Garrison talked about how, in her fight for women's rights, Susan B. Anthony had suffered ridicule and sneer, but she faced whatever was flung at her with "undaunted courage." He acknowledged the pain she'd suffered during the fury that erupted over whether to include women in the Fourteenth and Fifteenth Amendments. "Dissensions are inevitable in all human organizations, those of reform included," he said. "The wounds of the enemy are marks of honor, but those of fellow reformers pierce to the marrow. Nobody experienced these tribulations more than did this positive and self-reliant leader." When he mentioned that she'd also suffered from "misunderstood motive," he was perhaps offering an apology.

The final tribute was given by Anna Shaw, who said, "The ages to come will revere her name . . . Her work will not be finished, nor will her last word be spoken, while there remains a wrong to be righted or a fettered life to be freed in all the earth."

13
Legacy

During the years following Anthony's death, increasing numbers of women took to the streets and demanded the right to vote. When the United States entered World War I in 1917, the National American Woman Suffrage Association encouraged women to help with the war effort—just as the women's groups before the Civil War had thrown their support behind the Republicans and the Union. This time, though, the response was different. President Woodrow Wilson, who until then had been indifferent to the cause of

The Suffragist Parade in New York on May 4, 1914. Women marching for the right to vote adopted white as their color. Harris & Ewing, photographers.

women's suffrage, now took notice. "We have made partners of the women in this war," he said. "Shall we admit them only to a partnership of suffering and sacrifice and toil and not to a partnership of privilege and right?" In September of 1918, President Wilson asked the Senate to pass an amendment guaranteeing women the right to vote. Congress heeded his call and drafted the amendment, which stated simply that

> *The right of citizens of the United States to vote shall not be denied or abridged by the United States or by any State on account of sex.*
>
> *Congress shall have power to enforce this article by appropriate legislation.*

✯ ✯ ✯ ✯ ✯ ✯ ✯ ✯ ✯ ✯ ✯ ✯ ✯ ✯ ✯

By this time, women already had the right to vote in many of the states, although in some they had partial voting rights, for example, the right to vote in school elections or primaries. In addition, women had already won the right to vote in Australia, Austria, Canada, Great Britain, Czechoslovakia, Finland, Germany, Norway, the Soviet Union, and Poland. Since 1870 when the Fifteenth Amendment was passed, three other amendments had been added to the Constitution—one allowing a federal income tax, another concerning the selection of senators, and a third prohibiting the sale of alcohol. The amendment giving women the vote was thus the nineteenth. It was also called the Susan B. Anthony Amendment.

In the spring of 1919, the House and Senate passed the Nineteenth Amendment. The following year, Tennessee became the thirty-sixth state to ratify it, making the amendment part of the United States Constitution.

Anthony had imagined that when women were allowed to vote and thus had a voice in making the laws, the injustices women suffered would be righted. Instead, for forty years after the Nineteenth Amendment became part of the Constitution, not much changed. Women remained largely shut out of politics and the professions. Women's wages remained less than men's for the same work. Law enforcement turned a blind eye to wife beating. A married woman was not allowed to sign contracts or apply for loans or credit without her husband's written permission. The notion that women were intended to occupy the private sphere and not the public on the whole remained intact. A small percentage of women broke through what has been called the glass ceiling and made significant contributions to medicine, science, law, and other professions, but those were notable exceptions.

Legacy

Beginning in the second half of the twentieth century, a new movement arose, initially called Women's Liberation, and later called the Women's Movement. The word "feminist" came into use. This new wave of feminism had much in common with the movement of the nineteenth century. Women activists rebelled against restrictive clothing. They sought to free women from what they saw as an oppressive social structure. They demanded equal pay for equal work. They wanted tougher laws against wife beating. They wanted laws protecting women from harassment. They demanded complete equality with men. In short, everything Susan B. Anthony strove for, women in the second half of the twentieth century demanded.

As a result of the protests and demands of the 1960s and 1970s, women entered the professions in increasingly large numbers. Women became doctors, lawyers, judges, scientists, senators and congresswomen, governors, and business executives. By the end of the twentieth century, there were two women on the United States Supreme Court.

Just as there was a counter-suffrage movement in the nineteenth century, the late twentieth century also saw a conservative backlash to the women's movement. Leaders of this conservative

SUSAN B. ANTHONY

movement, such as Phyllis Schlafly (1924–2016), feared that liberating women would destroy the American family. Schlafly and others believed that women were the weaker sex, and in demanding equality, women were giving up the special privileges attached to womanhood, namely the chance to remain at home and care for children and family. In 2016, one of Phyllis Schlafly's final acts was to endorse conservative businessman Donald Trump for president.

Donald Trump's opponent, Hillary Clinton, was the first female presidential candidate nominated by a major political party. Like Susan B. Anthony, she was a reformer. She entered politics as a young woman immediately out of law school, working for civil rights for blacks, making sure black children were permitted to enroll in schools. While serving as first lady during Bill Clinton's presidency, she made a speech in Beijing declaring that women's rights were human rights.

When the 2016 votes were counted, Hillary Clinton received 48.2 percent of the popular vote. Donald Trump won 46.1 percent, with independent candidates making up the remainder. Although Clinton won almost three million more votes than her opponent, she lost the election. The reason: Elections are not decided by the popular vote; they are decided by the electoral

Legacy

college, a complex system of delegates selected by the states. Thus it is possible to earn more votes, but lose the election.

On Election Day 2016, hundreds of people—mostly women—visited the grave of Susan B. Anthony. They wanted to pay homage to the person who would have been thrilled to know that a woman was a serious contender for the presidency of the United States. It has become customary for voters at the polls to receive "I voted today" stickers. With what must have been feelings of reverence, joy, and gratitude, the visitors placed their "I voted" stickers on Susan B. Anthony's tombstone.

Susan B. Anthony's tombstone covered with "I voted today" stickers

Notes

Prologue: "The Times That Try Women's Souls"

1. "The Times That Try Women's Souls": Harper, *The Life and Work of Susan B. Anthony*, vol. 1 (Indianapolis: Bowen-Merril, 1899), 138.
2. "gives him the right . . . what she wants it for": Harper, vol. 1, 139.
3. "Here, take this child, I'm tired": Ibid.
3. "Well good folks . . . these surely are the times that try women's souls": Harper, *Life and Work*, vol. 1, 138.
4. "Women's subsistence . . . his consequent power": Harper, *Life and Work*, vol. 1, 385.
4. "Men their rights . . . nothing less": This was the motto used on the masthead of the *Revolution*, published by Susan B. Anthony and Elizabeth Cady Stanton after the Civil War.

1. A Quaker Girlhood

5. "I doubt if there be any mortal who clings to loves with greater tenacity than do I": Harper, *Life and Work*, vol. 1, 231.
8. "the torment of their lives . . . all generations": Harper, *Life and Work*, vol. 1, 70.
9. "I am sorry . . . revered the most": Harper, *Life and Work*, vol. 1, 72.
10. insisting that she wasn't "good" enough: Kathleen Barry, *Susan B. Anthony: A Biography of a Singular Feminist* (New York: New York University Press, 1988), 8.
14. "Grandma's potato . . . your boiled dinners!": Harper, *Life and Work*, vol. 1, 14.

Notes

15 "I'll tend your loom if you'll look after this": Alma Lutz, *Susan B. Anthony: Rebel, Crusader, Humanitarian* (Washington, D.C.: Zenger, 1959), 1.
16 "If Sally Ann knows . . . woman overseer in the mill": Ibid.
17 "I was much too serious . . . never failed her": *Leavenworth Weekly Times*, interview, November 16, 1899.
19 "Oh, what pangs . . . leave of him again": Lutz, *Susan B. Anthony*, 10.

2. The Financial Crisis

20 "I think the girl . . . very sweet": Harper, *Life and Work*, vol. 3, 1, 351.
21 "Five weeks . . . more watchful in the future": Harper, *Life and Work*, vol. 1, 27.
22 "Thy sister . . . thy capability": Lutz, *Susan B. Anthony*, 11.
24 "O can I ever forget . . . seems impossible": Ibid.
24 "happy moment": Harper, *Life and Work*, vol. 1, 34.
25 "O, that he may have the courage . . . scenes of life": Katharine Anthony, *Susan B. Anthony: Her Personal History and Her Era* (Garden City, NY: Doubleday, 1954), 50.
25–26 "I again left home . . . our business affairs": Harper, *Life and Work*, vol. 1, 34.
26–27 "Did a large washing . . . carpet yesterday": Harper, *Life and Work*, vol. 1, 36.
28 "The people about here are anti-abolitionist . . . told them to sit there": Harper, *Life and Work*, vol. 1, 39.
28 "Really, one would have thought . . . seen the commotion": Harper, *Life and Work*, vol. 1, 41.
29 "nothing more than ordinary men . . . any mortal being": Ibid.
29 "He had a slave . . . fine thing this freedom is!": Harper, *Life and Work*, vol. 1, 43.
30 "There is no reason . . . do both": Harper, *Life and Work*, vol. 1, 44.

Notes

3. An Unconventional Young Woman

32 "In those days . . . taken the consequences": Lynn Sherr, *Failure Is Impossible: Susan B. Anthony in Her Own Words* (New York: Times Books, 1995), 14.

35 "I am most happy . . . since this morning": Barry, *Susan B. Anthony*, 44.

35 "The scholars . . . backward if anything": Ibid.

36 "plaid, white, blue . . . deprived of a teacher": Ann D. Gordon, ed., *Selected Papers of Elizabeth Cady Stanton and Susan B. Anthony*, vol. 1 (Brunswick, NJ: Rutgers University Press, 2000), 53.

36 "real soft-headed old bachelor": Harper, *Life and Work*, vol. 1, 38.

36–37 "must have a total . . . fool of himself": Harper, *Life and Work*, vol. 1, 51. Also Geoffrey C. Ward and Ken Burns, *Not for Ourselves Alone: The Story of Elizabeth Cady Stanton and Susan B. Anthony* (New York: Knopf, 1999), 37.

37 "I can see in the mirror . . . flow of spirits": Barry, *Susan B. Anthony* 46.

38 "We hold these truths . . . created equal": Gordon, *Selected Papers*, vol. 1, 78.

40 "the day . . . half-inebriated seducer": Speech to the Daughters of Temperance, March 2, 1849. Gordon, *Selected Papers*, vol. 1, 136.

41 "I am tired of theory . . . watch word": Sherr, *Failure Is Impossible*, 48.

41 "Oh . . . natural consequence": Harper, *Life and Work*, vol. 1, 52.

42 "It seems to me . . . I mingle": May 11, 1849. Gordon, *Selected Papers*, vol. 1, 146.

42 "drawbacks to marriage . . . remain single": Harper, *Life and Work*, vol. 1, 52.

43 "I'm sure no man . . . I have been": Sherr, *Failure Is Impossible*, 6.

Notes

43 "Being a Quakeress . . . good mistress for a (house)": Sherr, *Failure Is Impossible*, 13.

43 "slip easily into submission and dependence": Barry, *Susan B. Anthony*, 38.

43–44 "I would not consent . . . my own sex": Elizabeth Cady Stanton, *A Brief Biography of Susan B. Anthony*, Kindle edition (New York: A. J. Cornell, 2011), location 132.

4. All the Good You Can

45 "It is only through . . . make them any better": Harper, *Life and Work*, vol. 2, 572.

46 "Miss Anthony . . . in Canajoharie": Harper, *Life and Work*, vol. 1, 54.

47 "N— printing press": *Union and Advertiser*, Rochester, New York; Feb. 21, 1894.

49 "strong-minded woman": Harper, *Life and Work*, vol. 1, 84.

49 "the perfection of common sense": Barry, *Susan B. Anthony*, 102.

49 "pleasing rather than pretty . . . expressive countenance": Harper, *Life and Work*, vol. 2, 124.

49 "Go do all the good you can": Harper, *Life and Work*, vol. 1, 518.

55 "If the Bible teaches . . . gadding around the country": Barry, *Susan B. Anthony*, 105

55 "How well I remember . . . I do not know": Elizabeth Cady Stanton et. al., *History of Woman Suffrage*, vol 1. (Rochester, NY: Charles Man, 1887), 457.

5. A Nation in Need of Reform

57 "Our mission . . . conscience of the North": Sherr, *Failure Is Impossible*, 33.

58–59 "That man over there . . . arn't I a woman?": Available here: www.blackpast.org/1851-sojourner-truth-arnt-i-woman.

Notes

59 "was black and she was a woman . . . calm and dignified": Stanton et. al., *History of Woman Suffrage*, vol. 1, 567.

59 "Tomfoolery . . . shudder to hear": Harper, *Life and Work*, vol. 1, 77–78.

59 "How did woman . . . doomed to subjection": Harper, *Life and Work*, vol. 1, 78.

62 "I will gladly . . . as you desire": Gordon, *Selected Papers*, vol. 1, 197.

64 "With the cares of a large family . . . selfishness:" Elizabeth Cady Stanton, *Eighty Years and More: Memoirs of Elizabeth Cady Stanton, 1815–1897* (New York: T. Fisher Unwin, 1898; Kindle edition, New York: Madison and Adams, 2018), location 1,925.

64 "It was mid such exhilarating scenes . . . constitutional arguments": *Eighty Years and More*, location 1, 917.

64 "that stately Quaker girl": Stanton, *Memoirs*, 1928.

65 "My heart was filled with grief . . . assigned to them": Harper, *Life and Work*, vol. 1, 98.

65–66 "Mr. President . . . future Presidents, Senators, and Congressmen": This entire incident, with quotations, is given in Sherr, *Failure Is Impossible*, 19–20.

67 "profoundest silence": Sherr, *Failure Is Impossible*, 20.

67 "I felt so mortified . . . swallow me up": Harper, *Life and Work*, vol. 1, 98–99.

67 "I have been asked . . . pedestals into the dust": Ibid.

67 "The attention of my audience . . . instead of my words": Ward and Burns, *Not for Ourselves Alone*, 71.

68 "true woman . . . insinuating manners": Carol Hymowitz and Michaele Weissman, *A History of Women in America* (New York: Bantam, 1978), location 148.

69 "be her own individual . . . wisdom and strength": Barry, *Susan B.*

Anthony, 115.

69 "use, worthily . . . herself and the race": Barry, *Susan B. Anthony*, 115.

69 "embarked in an unpopular cause and must be content to row upstream": Belle Squire, *The Woman Movement in America: A Short Account of the Struggle for Equal Rights* (Chicago: A. C. McClurg, 1911), 86.

69 "for future generations must we labor": Harper, *Life and Work*, vol. 1, 405.

69–70 "I have *very weak* moments . . . I feel *alone*": Gordon, *Selected Papers*, 353. Emphasis in the original.

71 "blood chilled . . . degrading influence": Barry, *Susan B. Anthony*, 90.

71 "Oh, Slavery, hateful thing that thou art thus to blunt the keen edge of conscience": Harper, *Life and Work*, vol. 1, 118.

72 "We ask you to feel . . . in his fellowman": Harper, *Life and Work*, vol. 1, 153.

72 "What is to be done with the freed slaves . . . oppressors for centuries": Sherr, *Failure Is Impossible*, 33.

73–74 "We cheerfully pay your expenses and want to keep you at the head of the work": Harper, *Life and Work*, vol. 1, 154.

74 "wisely and efficiently": Harper, *Life and Work*, vol. 1, 165–166.

75 "That the exclusion . . . mean and cruel": Harper, *Life and Work*, vol. 1, 155.

76 "vast social evil": Ibid.

76 "I did indeed see by the papers . . . educational convention": Ibid.

6. Civil War

77 "Organize, agitate, educate must be our war cry": Harper, *Life and Work*, vol. 2, 741.

82 "The child belongs . . . back to the asylum": Stanton, *Reminiscences*,

Notes

location 2,493.

80–81 "Could the dark secrets . . . made by men for women": Stanton, *Memoirs*, location 2492.

83 "abducted a man's child and must surrender it": Harper, *Life and Work*, vol. 1, 208.

83 "outrage . . . and you also": Ibid.

84 "hasty and ill-judged": Gordon, *Selected Papers*, vol. 1, 458.

84–85 "All I have done . . . to its father": This entire anecdote is recounted in Sherr, *Failure Is Impossible*, 214.

85 "Very many abolitionists . . . women's rights": Ward and Burns, *Not for Ourselves Alone*, 95.

85 "You are not married . . . lecturing on slavery": Sherr, *Failure Is Impossible*, 214.

85–86 "put a word on paper . . . stand by you": Barry, *Susan B. Anthony*, 144.

87 "Rotten eggs were thrown . . . every direction": Harper, *Life and Work*, vol. 1, 211.

87 "damned abolitionists": Harper, *Life and Work*, vol. 1, 210.

87 "pestiferous fanatic": Anthony, *Susan B. Anthony*, 149.

88 "Why, boys . . . before a Grand Jury": Faye E. Dudden, *Fighting Chance: The Struggle over Women Suffrage and Black Suffrage in Reconstruction America* (New York: Oxford University Press, 2011), 48.

88 "the Constitution as it is . . . peace and prosperity": Harper, *Life and Work*, vol. 1, 228.

88 "I ask you . . . from the beginning": Susan B. Anthony, "Return to the 'Old Union'" speech, 1863.

89 "I wish the government . . . merciless war": Gordon, *Selected Papers*, vol. 1, 475.

90 "All alike say . . . all our best friends": Gordon, *Selected Papers*, vol. 1, 475.

Notes

90 "While the old guard sleeps . . . snatched from us": Ibid.
91 "blunder . . . against the world": Barry, *Susan B. Anthony*, 149.
91 "Oh, this babydom . . . engaged in it": Sherr, *Failure Is Impossible*, 9.
95 "felt the foundation . . . stunned and helpless": Harper, *Life and Work*, vol. 1, 224.
95 "a shock not easily or soon to be recovered from": Gordon, *Selected Papers*, vol. 1, 478.

7. Emancipation

96 "The principle of self-government . . . incident of birth": Harper, *Life and Work*, vol. 2, 1001.
97 "all slaves, all citizens . . . shall be practically established": Dudden, *Fighting Chance*, 51.
97–98 "In a true democracy . . . representation in that government": Ibid.
98 "Go to the rich . . . feet of Congress" Squire, *Woman Movement*, 120.
98 "rise up . . . consciences for approval": Gordon, *Selected Papers*, vol. 1, 492.
99 "Well, Miss Anthony, you're the most audacious beggar I ever heard": Stanton, *Brief Biography*, location 95.
101 "These are terrible times": Harper, *Life and Work*, vol. 1, 230.
101 "a mighty army, one hundred thousand strong, without arms or banners": Available here: www.senate.gov/artandhistory/history/common/civil_war/WomensNationalLoyalLeague.htm.
102 "Neither slavery . . . appropriate legislation": Available here: www.law.cornell.edu/constitution/amendmentxiii
104 "principle force behind the drive for the Thirteenth Amendment": From the U.S. Senate information page: www.senate.gov/artandhistory/history/common/civil_war/WomensNationalLoyalLeague.htm.

Notes

105 "burning, blistering shame": Harper, *Life and Work*, vol. 1, 243.
106 "Morning telegram . . . sworn in": Gordon, *Selected Papers*, vol. 1, 542.
107 "I have argued constantly . . . deep water": Stanton, *Letters*, vol. 2, 105.
108 "I hope some day . . . exclusively to the Negro": Phillips, speech at the May 9, 1865, Anti-Slavery Society meeting.
108 "impertinent": Barry, *Susan B. Anthony*, 168.
108 "Dear Friend . . . entirely of males?": Stanton, *Letters*, vol. 2, 104–105.
108 "Come back and help. There will be a room for you": Stanton, *Letters*, vol. 2, 105.

8. We the People

109 "It was we the people . . . formed the Union": Susan B. Anthony, "Women's Right to Vote" speech, 1873.
112 "enclosed in the same dark dungeon": Vorenberg, *Final Freedom*, 82.
113 "No state shall . . . provisions of this article": Available here: www.law.cornell.edu/constitution/amendmentxiiii.
114 "If that word 'male' be inserted, it will take us a century at least to get it out": Brenda Wineapple, "Ladies Last," *The American Scholar*, summer 2013.
115 "woman" was "in thrall to fashion": Dudden, *Fighting Chance*, 84.
115 "corrupting the channels of politics": Dudden, *Fighting Chance*, 84.
115 "No ballot box . . . reform yourselves": Ibid.
116 "one grand, distinctive, national idea—Universal Suffrage": Stanton, *History of Woman Suffrage*, vol. 6, 172.
117 "cut off her right hand than ask the ballot for the black man and not for woman": Harper, *Life and Work*, vol. 1, 261.
117 "most inopportune": Harper, *Life and Work*, vol. 1, 265.
117 "The insertion of that word . . . question settled": Lutz, *Susan B. Anthony*, location 3, 171.
119 "duty . . . for the colored men": Harper, *Life and Work*, vol. 1, 268.
120 "There is a great stir . . . as it was before": Dudden, *Fighting Chance*,

Notes

96.
121 "[Colored women] go out washing . . . nobody speaks for them": Ibid.
121 "All I ask for myself . . . everlasting principle": Stanton, *History of Woman Suffrage*, vol. 2, 220.
122 "I am an anti-slavery man . . . which they are subjected?": Harper, *Life and Work*, vol. 1, 257–58.
122 "give their influence . . . against the equality of women": Dudden, *Fighting Chance*, 93.
123 "thankful in my soul if *any*body can get out of this black pit": *History of Woman Suffrage*, vol. 2, 384.
123 "the colored man . . . left to serve": Dudden, *Fighting Chance*, 185–86.
123 "As much as white women need the ballot, colored women need it more": Rosalyn Terborg-Penn, *African American Women in the Struggle for the Vote* (Bloomington, IN: Indiana University Press, 1998), 47.
124 "Mrs. Elizabeth Cady Stanton . . . are on your heels": Dudden, *Fighting Chance*, 91.
125 "Four million Southern women will counterbalance four million Negro men and women": Dudden, *Fighting Chance*, 93.

9. Betrayal

126 "Cautious, careful . . . can never effect a reform": Harper, *Life and Work*, vol. 1, 197.
127 "every old maid to vote": Dudden, *Fighting Chance*, 129.
127 "their pretended champions . . . worst enemies": Dudden, *Fighting Chance*, 124–25.
127 "squelch the black-versus-women story": Dudden, *Fighting Chance*, 125.
127 "stop asking about equal rights . . . daughters also": Ibid.
129 The plan backfired spectactularly: Barry, *Susan B. Anthony*, 181, and Dudden, *Fighting Chance*, 108–32.

Notes

129 "loaded down" and "side issue": Dudden, *Fighting Chance*, 134.

131 "fighting chance": A premise of scholar and historian Faye Dudden's book, *Fighting Chance*, is that Stanton and Anthony rejected the claim that women's rights had no hope of succeeding. They believed they had a fighting chance and acted accordingly.

133 "Mr. Garrison always was . . . through his spectacles": Barry, *Susan B. Anthony*, 198.

133 "despotic in spirit and purpose": Ibid.

134 "man's government . . . male and female, black and white": *The Revolution*, December 24, 1868.

135 "exalting the son over the mother . . . moral power to brute force": Gordon, *Selected Papers*, vol. 2, 194–95.

135 "The male element . . . and death": Ibid.

135 "Men need refining . . . better than man": *Revolution*, Jan. 17, 1868, available here: archive.org/stream /revolution-1868-01-22/1868-01-22_djvu.txt.

135–136 "two million . . . and ignorant": Wineapple, "Ladies Last."

136 "culminate in fearful outrages . . . Southern states": Stanton et. al. *History of Woman Suffrage*, vol. 3, 641.

137 "when there were few houses . . . Mrs. Elizabeth Cady Stanton": Sherr, *Failure Is Impossible*, 40.

137 "These two women were determined . . . won *yesterday*": Dudden, *Fighting Chance*, 142.

139 "moderate correction": *Rhodes v. North Carolina*, 61 N.C. 453, 1868.

139 "Every household . . . and condition": *Rhodes v. North Carolina*, 61 N.C. 453 (1868).

140 "appeared still unable to comprehend . . . her probable death": Gordon, *Selected Papers*, vol. 2, 158.

140 "Men have made the law cunningly for their own protection": Gordon, *Selected Papers*, vol. 2, 191.

Notes

140 "satisfy the public list . . . hanging a few women": Barry, *Susan B. Anthony*, 217.

141–142 "attempted to force . . . without delay": Harper, *Life and Work*, vol. 1, 323.

142 "The question of precedence . . . should be enfranchised": Gordon, *Selected Papers*, vol. 2, 238.

142 "If Mr. Douglass had noticed who clapped . . . they were all men": Gordon, *Selected Papers*, vol. 2, 239.

142–143 "I do not see . . . Is that not true about black women": Sherr, *Failure Is Impossible*, 40.

143 "Yes, yes . . . because she is black": Ibid.

143 "in respect to the nature of our sexes": Gordon, *Selected Papers*, vol. 2, 240.

143 "it will place her . . . that is needed": Ibid.

143–144 "wasn't equal rights . . . men by their sides": Sherr, *Failure Is Impossible*, 41.

144 "Neither . . . upon an Equal Rights platform": Gordon, *Selected Papers*, vol. 2, 240–241.

144 "This howl comes from the men . . . out of marriage": Harper, *Life and Work*, vol. 1, 325.

145 "some insist . . . finance, labor, and capital": Gordon, *Selected Papers*, vol. 2, 293.

146 "radical egalitarian": Kathleen L. Barry, "Susan B. Anthony: Radical Egalitarian of Women's Rights," *Women Public Speakers in the United States, 1800–1925*, ed. Campbell, Karlyn Korhs (Westport, CT: Greenwood Press, 1993).

10. Let the World Wag

148 "How do I keep so energetic? . . . any form of self-absorption": Sherr, *Failure Is Impossible*, 241.

Notes

150 "If all the men . . . no Laura Fair in jail tonight": Harper, *Life and Work*, vol. 1, 391.

150 "I declare to you . . . there I take my stand": Harper, *Life and Work*, vol. 1, 392.

151 "never before got such a raking": Harper, *Life and Work*, vol. 2, 434.

151 "It is scandalous . . . let the world wag": Barry, *Susan B. Anthony*, 239.

151 "strident spinster": Barry, *Susan B. Anthony*, 102.

151–152 "Ask nine men out of ten . . . but hate of men": Ibid.

152 "We could not help thinking . . . in her younger days": Ward and Burns, *Not for Ourselves Alone*, 138.

152–153 "I could never see how . . . to lecture married woman": Sherr, *Failure Is Impossible*, 180–181.

153 "If women do not desire . . . degraded by its deprivation": Harper, *Life and Work*, vol. 1, 263.

154 "ablest constitutional lawyers in the country": Harper, *Life and Work*, vol. 1, 409.

155 "Now register . . . remaining opportunities": Harper, *Life and Work*, vol. 1, 423.

156 "Well, I have been . . . I hope you voted, too": Gordon, *Selected Papers*, vol. 2, 524

157 "Is it a crime for a United States citizen to vote?": Gordon, *Selected Papers*, vol. 2, 554.

157–159 "corruptionist . . . enactment of a comedy": Harper, *Life and Work*, vol. 1, 436.

159 "outrage": Gordon, *Selected Papers*, vol. 2, 611.

160 "sublime silence": Barry, *Susan B. Anthony*, 255.

160 "Yes, Your Honor . . . no jury of my peers, but I have had no jury at all": *Selected Papers*, vol. 2, 613.

160 "Sit down . . . rendered by law." Gordon, *Selected Papers*,

vol. 2, 613.

160 "Yes, but laws made by men . . . for the benefit benefit of men.": Ibid.
161 "My friends . . . participate in that government": Gordon, *Selected Papers*, vol. 3, 23.
161 "dear elder sister . . . cradled together": Barry, *Susan B. Anthony*, 257.
163–164 "The natural and proper timidity . . . of womanhood": *Minor v. Happerset*, 88 U.S. 162, 1875.
164 "The paramount destiny . . . upon exceptional cases": *Minor v. Happerset*, 88 U.S. 162, 1864.
164 "clowns . . . laws for queens": Gordon, *Selected Papers*, vol. 4, 91.
165 "While the Nation is buoyant . . . country's birth": Gordon, *Selected Papers*, vol. 3, 234.
165 "Yet we cannot forget . . . degradation of disenfranchisement": Ibid.
166 "others more brave and determined . . . make it a historical document": Ibid.
166 "face paled, as bowing low, he received the declaration": Harper, *Life and Work*, vol. 1, 478.

11. A New Generation

168 "We shall someday . . . handful of women of the past": Anthony's address at the National-American Convention of 1894. Sherr, *Failure Is Impossible*, xi.
168 "Men have been faithful . . . the other half": Harper, *Life and Work*, vol. 3, 542.
169 "It makes me sad and tired . . . for the rest of my life": Barry, *Susan B. Anthony*, 272.
170 "It was difficult . . . hurl my manuscript at his head": Ward and Burns, *Not for Ourselves Alone*, 155.
172 "in all matters connected with women she has been very conservative": Barry, *Susan B. Anthony*, 329.

Notes

172 "Miss Anthony the London Sensation . . . an innovation": Sherr, *Failure Is Impossible*, 310.

173 "It is well for us . . . exile in Siberia": Sherr, *Failure Is Impossible*, 118.

177-179 "but for the suffrage movement . . . the things we pray for": Sherr, *Failure Is Impossible*, 185.

179 "I tried to assure her . . . Abraham's bosom": Gordon, *Selected Papers*, vol. 5, XXIII.

179 "It is better to be . . . friend than his echo": Harper, *Life and Work*, vol. 3, 1258

179 "at the point of the bayonet": Barry, *Susan B. Anthony*, 286.

181 "Why don't they kick the ball . . . silly, not brutal": Sherr, *Failure Is Impossible*, 284.

181-183 "a great deal to emancipate . . . they had votes": Sherr, *Failure Is Impossible*, 277.

183 "continually exploring new fields for missionary labors": Stanton, *Memoirs*, location 1,926.

183 "They let the girls in—said there was no alternative": Sherr, *Failure Is Impossible*, 27.

183 "I feel it would be just as well if I reached the end on cars": Harper, *Life and Work*, vol. 3, 1,360.

183-184 "I am not retiring . . . do not do it well." Harper, *Life and Work*, vol. 3, 1170.

184 "I suppose at eighty-one . . . change come over us": Barry, *Susan B. Anthony*, 335.

184 "Oh, if I could but . . . all the works for women!" Harper, *Life and Work*, vol. 2, 667

184-185 "We little dreamed . . . fifty years ago": Gordon, *Selected Papers*, vol. 6, 217.

185 "Mother passed away today": Gordon, *Selected Papers*, vol. 6, 218.

185 "the climax of my career": Ward and Burns, *Not for Ourselves*

Notes

Alone, 210.

186–187 "The face is wrinkled now . . . absolutely tireless": interview, *Leavenworth Weekly Times*, November 16, 1899.

187 "wives, as mothers . . . Great Emancipator": Details of this entire interview are given in Harper, *Life and Work*, vol. 3, 1376.

187–188 "Ridiculous . . . keep the boys in the cradle always": Sherr, *Failure Is Impossible*, 143–44.

188 "This is rather different . . . were not roses": Harper, *Life and Work*, vol. 3, 68.

189 "hearty good wishes . . . honorable life." Harper, *Life and Work*, vol. 3, 1407–8.

189 "I wish men would do something . . . than to praise me endlessly": Ward and Burnes, *Not for Ourselves Alone*, 211.

190 "They are still passing . . . sacrifices they have made": Barry, *Susan B. Anthony*, 355–56.

190 "When it is a funeral . . . go on with the work": Quoted here: susanbanthonyhouse.org/blog/remember-susan-b-anthony-on-march-13.

Afterward

192 "undaunted courage": Harper, *Life and Work*, vol. 3, 1,435.

192 "Dissensions are inevitable . . . self-reliant leader": Ibid.

192 "The ages to come . . . freed in all the earth": Harper, *Life and Work*, vol. 3, 1,440.

Legacy

195 "We have made partners . . . privilege and right": Quotation available here: www.senate.gov/artandhistory/history/minute/A_Vote_For_Women.htm.

Time Line

1817 ✯ Lucy Read marries Daniel Anthony.

1820 ✯ **FEBRUARY 15:** Susan B. Anthony is born.

1826 ✯ The Anthony family moves to Battenville, New York, so Daniel Anthony can pursue business opportunities.

1837 ✯ The depression causes Daniel Anthony's business to fail.

1838 ✯ Anthony leaves the Deborah Moulson Female Academy and returns home.

1845 ✯ The Anthony family moves to Rochester, New York, and becomes involved with anti-slavery activists.

1846 ✯ Anthony takes the position of headmistress at Canajoharie Academy.

1849 ✯ Anthony resigns her position at the Canajoharie Academy and returns to her family's Rochester farm.

1851 ✯ Anthony meets Elizabeth Cady Stanton.

1856 ✯ Anthony begins work for the American Anti-Slavery Society.

1860 ✯ **NOVEMBER 6:** Abraham Lincoln is elected president.

1861 ✯ **APRIL 12:** Confederate artillery fires on Fort Sumter; the Civil War begins.

1862 ✯ **APRIL:** Lincoln emancipates the slaves in Washington, D.C.

✯ **JULY:** Lincoln announces the Emancipation Proclamation.

✯ **NOVEMBER 25:** Daniel Anthony dies.

Time Line

1863 ✦ MAY 14: Anthony and Stanton form a new organization, the Women's Loyal National League, to help pass the Thirteenth Amendment, abolishing slavery.

1865 ✦ JANUARY 31: The House of Representatives passes the Thirteenth Amendment.

1866 ✦ JUNE 13: Senator Bingham presents the Fourteenth Amendment to Congress. Anthony and Stanton object to the word "male" used to designate voters.

1867 ✦ Anthony and Stanton go to Kansas, where there is a ballot initiative to put women on the ballot.

1868 ✦ Anthony and Stanton begin publishing their newspaper, the *Revolution*. Anthony forms the Working Women's Association for women laborers.

1869 ✦ Congress passes the Fifteenth Amendment. The women's group splits into two separate groups, the American Woman Suffrage Association, which endorses the amendment even though women are excluded, and the National Woman Suffrage Association (led by Anthony and Stanton), which does not.

1872 ✦ Anthony is arrested for voting.

1873 ✦ Anthony is tried and found guilty of voting illegally.

1875 ✦ The Supreme Court rules that the Fourteenth Amendment does not guarantee voting rights to women (*Minor v. Happersett*).

1876 ✦ JULY 4: Anthony hands out copies of the "Declaration of Rights of the Women of the United States" at Philadelphia's centennial celebration.

Time Line

1881 ✦ Anthony, Stanton, and Matilda Joslin Gage publish volume I of the *History of Woman Suffrage*. They publish volumes II, III, and IV in 1882, 1885, and 1902.

1890 ✦ The two women's organizations merge and call themselves the National American Woman Suffrage Association.

1898 ✦ *The Life and Work of Susan B. Anthony: Including Public Addresses, Her Own Letters, and Many from Her Contemporaries during Fifty Years. A Story of the Evolution of the Status of Women* is published. Anthony establishes a press bureau to feed articles on women's suffrage to the national and local press.

1905 ✦ Anthony meets with President Theodore Roosevelt about a constitutional amendment allowing women to vote; he is not interested.

1906 ✦ **MARCH 13**: Anthony dies at her Rochester home.

1920 ✦ The Nineteenth Amendment to the U.S. Constitution, also called the Susan B. Anthony Amendment, becomes part of the U.S. Constitution, granting the right to vote to all women over the age of twenty-one.

Selected Writings of Susan B. Anthony

Anthony's 1863 antislavery speech, "Return to the 'Old Union'"

There is great fear expressed on all sides lest this war shall be made a war for the Negro. I am willing that it shall be. It is a war to found an empire on the Negro in slavery, and shame on us if we do not make it a war to establish the Negro in freedom–against whom the whole nation, North and South, East and West, in one mighty conspiracy, has combined from the beginning. Instead of suppressing the real cause of the war, it should have been proclaimed, not only by the people, but by the President, Congress, Cabinet, and every military commander. Instead of President Lincoln's waiting two long years before calling to the side of the Government the four millions of allies whom we have had within the territory of rebeldom, it should have been the first decree he sent forth.

Every hour's delay, every life sacrificed up to the proclamation that called the slave to freedom and to arms, was nothing less than downright murder by the Government...

We talk about returning to the old Union–"the Union as it was," and "the Constitution as it is"–about "restoring our country to peace and prosperity—to the blessed conditions that existed before the war!" I ask you what sort of peace, what sort of prosperity, have we had? Since the first slave-ship sailed up the James River with its human cargo, and there, on the soil of the Old Dominion, sold it to the highest bidder, we have had nothing but war. When that pirate captain landed on the shores of Africa, and there kidnapped the first stalwart Negro, and fastened the first manacle, the struggle between that captain and that Negro was the commencement of the terrible war in the midst of which we are to-day. Between the slave and the master there has been war, and war only. This is only a new form of it.

No, no; we ask for no return to the old conditions. We ask for something better. We want a Union that is a Union in fact, a Union in spirit, not a sham. (Applause). By the Constitution as it is, the North has stood pledged to protect slavery in the States where it existed. We have been bound, in case of insurrections, to go to the aid, not of those struggling for liberty, but of the oppressors. It was politicians who made this pledge at the beginning, and who have renewed it from year to year to this day. These same men have had control of the churches, the Sabbath-schools, and all religious influences; and the women have been a party in complicity with slavery . . .

Woman must now assume her God-given responsibilities, and make herself what she is clearly designed to be, the educator of the race. Let her no longer be the mere reflector, the echo of the worldly pride and ambition of man. Had the women of the North studied to know and to teach their sons the law of justice to the black man, regardless of the frown or the smile of pro-slavery priest and politician, they would not now be called upon to offer the loved of their households to the bloody Moloch of war. And now, women of the North, I ask you to rise up with earnest, honest purpose, and go forward in the way of right, fearlessly, as independent human beings, responsible to God alone for the discharge of every duty, for the faithful use of every gift, the good Father has given you. Forget conventionalisms; forget what the world will say, whether you are in your place or out of your place; think your best thoughts, speak your best words, do your best works, looking to your own conscience for approval.

Susan B. Anthony on the Fifteenth Amendment, October 7, 1869, the Revolution

The *Revolution* criticizes, "opposes" the Fifteenth Amendment, not for what it is, but for what it is not. Not because it enfranchises black men, but because it does not enfranchise all women, black and white. It is not the little good it proposes, but the greater evil it perpetuates that we depreciate. It is not that in the abstract we do not rejoice that black men are to become the equals of white men, but that we deplore the fact that two million black women, hitherto the political and social equals of the men by their sides, are to become subject, slaves of these men. Our protest is not that all men are lifted out of the degradation of disenfranchisement, but that all women are left in.

Anthony's Woman's Suffrage Speech, 1873

Friends and fellow citizens: I stand before you tonight under indictment for the alleged crime of having voted at the last presidential election, without having a lawful right to vote. It shall be my work this evening to prove to you that in thus voting, I not only committed no crime, but, instead, simply exercised my citizen's rights, guaranteed to me and all United States citizens by the National Constitution, beyond the power of any state to deny.

The preamble of the Federal Constitution says:

We, the people of the United States, in order to form a more perfect union, establish justice, insure domestic tranquility, provide for the common defense, promote the general welfare, and secure the blessings of liberty to ourselves and our posterity, do ordain and establish this Constitution for the United States of America.

It was we, the people; not we, the white male citizens; nor yet we, the male citizens; but we, the whole people, who formed the Union. And we formed it, not to give the blessings of liberty, but to secure them; not to the half of ourselves and the half of our posterity, but to the whole people—women as well as men. And it

Selected Writings of Susan B. Anthony

is a downright mockery to talk to women of their enjoyment of the blessings of liberty while they are denied the use of the only means of securing them provided by this democratic-republican government—the ballot.

... To them this government has no just powers derived from the consent of the governed. To them this government is not a democracy. It is not a republic. It is an odious aristocracy; a hateful oligarchy of sex; the most hateful aristocracy ever established on the face of the globe; an oligarchy of wealth, where the rich govern the poor. An oligarchy of learning, where the educated govern the ignorant, or even an oligarchy of race, where the Saxon rules the African, might be endured; but this oligarchy of sex, which makes father, brothers, husband, sons, the oligarchs over the mother and sisters, the wife and daughters, of every household—which ordains all men sovereigns, all women subjects, carries dissension, discord, and rebellion into every home of the nation ...

The only question left to be settled now is: Are women persons? And I hardly believe any of our opponents will have the hardihood to say they are not. Being persons, then, women are citizens; and no state has a right to make any law, or to enforce any old law, that shall abridge their privileges or immunities. Hence, every discrimination against women in the constitutions and laws of the several states is today null and void, precisely as is every one against Negroes.

Bibliography

A Note on the Primary Sources

Ida Husted Harper worked closely with Susan B. Anthony to write an authorized biography, the first two volumes of which were published under Anthony's direction and with full access to all of Anthony's papers and letters. To ensure accuracy, Anthony requested back from people many of the letters she had written to them. When the biography was completed, Husted burned many of Anthony's original papers, because she wanted her biography to remain the authoritative one.

However, many of Anthony's original letters, diaries, and papers do survive and are available on microfilm from the Library of Congress. *The Papers of Elizabeth Cady Stanton and Susan B. Anthony*, edited by Patricia Holland and Ann D. Gordon, was published on microfilm, in fifty-three reels, in 1991. A large sampling of Anthony's letters, diaries, and speeches are available in the six volumes of *Selected Papers of Elizabeth Cady Stanton and Susan B. Anthony*, but they represent only a small percentage of the existing documents. The introductions to these volumes are invaluable.

Lynn Sherr's *Failure Is Impossible: Susan B. Anthony in Her Own Words* is a delightful collection of Anthony's speeches, letters, and diary entries. This volume, however, offers a small sampling. Thus there is still much scholarly work to be done in compiling a complete collected works of Susan B. Anthony.

Primary Sources and Internet Resources

Anthony, Susan B. "Return to the 'Old Union'" speech, 1863. Available here: susanbanthonyhouse.org/blog/wp-content/uploads/2017/07/Susan-B-Anthony-1863.pdf.

Bibliography

———. "The Status of Women, Past, Present, and Future." *The Arena*, May 1897.

———. "Women's Right to Vote" speech, 1873. Available here: sourcebooks.fordham.edu/mod/1873anthony.asp.

United States Constitution. Full text available here: www.law.cornell.edu/constitution/overview.

George Washington to Robert Morris, April 12, 1786. Available here: founders.archives.gov/documents/Washington/04-04-02-0019.

The Revolution, edited by Elizabeth Cady Stanton, is available here: archive.org/stream/revolution-1868-01-22/1868-01-22_djvu.txt.

Sherr, Lynn. *Failure Is Impossible: Susan B. Anthony in Her Own Words*. New York: Times Books, 1995.

Selected Papers of Elizabeth Cady Stanton and Susan B. Anthony, vol. 1: *In the School of Anti-Slavery, 1840–1866*. Ann D. Gordon, ed. New Brunswick, NJ: Rutgers University Press, 1997.

Selected Papers of Elizabeth Cady Stanton and Susan B. Anthony, vol. 2: *Against an Aristocracy of Sex, 1866–1873*. Ann D. Gordon, ed. New Brunswick, NJ: Rutgers University Press, 2000.

Selected Papers of Elizabeth Cady Stanton and Susan B. Anthony, vol. 3: *National Protections for National Citizens, 1873–1880*. Ann D. Gordon, ed. New Brunswick, NJ: Rutgers University Press, 2003.

Selected Papers of Elizabeth Cady Stanton and Susan B. Anthony, vol. 4: *When Clowns Make Laws for Queens, 1873–1880*. Ann D. Gordon, ed. New Brunswick, NJ: Rutgers University Press, 2006.

Susan B. Anthony House website: susanbanthonyhouse.org.

Truth, Sojourner. "Ar'nt I a Woman" speech, 1851. Available here: blackpast.org/1851-sojourner-truth-arnt-i-woman.

United States Senate website: www.senate.gov.

Phillips, Wendell. "The Former National Purpose. Two Years After. The New President." Speech, May 9, 1865. Important Session of the

Anti-Slavery Society, available here: www.nytimes.com/1865/05/10
/news/anniversaries-important-session-antislavery-society
-speeches-wendell-phillips.html?pagewanted=all.

Books

Anthony, Katharine. *Susan B. Anthony: Her Personal History and Her Era.* Garden City, NY: Doubleday, 1954.

Barry, Kathleen. *Susan B. Anthony: A Biography of a Singular Feminist.* New York: New York University Press, 1988.

Dudden, Faye E. *Fighting Chance: The Struggle over Woman Suffrage and Black Suffrage in Reconstruction America.* New York: Oxford University Press, 2011.

Harper, Ida Husted. *The Life and Work of Susan B. Anthony* (vols. 1–3), *Including Public Addresses, Her Own Letters, and Many from her Contemporaries During Fifty Years.* Indianapolis: Bowen-Merril, 1899. Vol. 1 available here: www.gutenberg.org/files/15220/15220-h/15220-h.htm. Vol. 2 available here: www.gutenberg.org/files/31125/31125-h/31125-h.htm. Vol. 3 available here: archive.org/details/lifeandworksusa02harpgoog.

Hymowitz, Carol and Michaele Weissman. *A History of Women in America.* New York: Bantam, 1978.

Lutz, Alma. *Susan B. Anthony: Rebel, Crusader, Humanitarian.* Zenger Publishing Co., Washington, D.C.: Zenger, 1959. Available here: www.gutenberg.org/files/20439/20439-h/20439-h.htm#Footnote_1_1 and archive.org/details/susanbanthonyreb00lutz.

Packard, Elizabeth Parsons Ware. *Modern Persecution or Insane Asylums Unveiled.* New York: Pelletreau & Raynor, 1873. Available here: archive.org/stream/39002086347219.med.yale.edu#page/n9/mode/2up/search/Picture.

Squire, Belle. *The Woman Movement in America: A Short Account of the*

Bibliography

Struggle for Equal Rights. Chicago: A. C. McClurg, 1911. Available here: archive.org/stream/womanmovementina00squirich#page/n11/mode/2up.

Stanton, Elizabeth Cady. *The Memoirs of Elizabeth Cady Stanton: Eighty Years and More, 1815–1897.* New York: T. Fisher Unwin, 1898. Kindle edition.

———. *A Brief Biography of Susan B. Anthony.* Originally published in 1884 as a portion of *Our Famous Women: An Authorized Record of Their Lives and Deeds.* Kindle edition. New York: A. J. Cornell, 2011.

Stanton, Elizabeth Cady, Susan B. Anthony, and Matilda Josyln Gage. *History of Woman Suffrage,* vols. 1–6. Rochester, NY: Charles Man, 1887.

Stanton, Theodore and Harriot Stanton Blanch, eds. *Elizabeth Cady Stanton: As Revealed in Her Letters, Diary, and Reminiscences.* Vols. I and II. New York: Harper & Brothers, 1902.

Terborg-Penn, Rosalyn. *African American Women in the Struggle for the Vote.* Bloomington, IN: Indiana University Press, 1998.

Ward, Geoffrey C. and Ken Burns. *Not for Ourselves Alone: The Story of Elizabeth Cady Stanton and Susan B. Anthony.* Based on a documentary film by Ken Burns and Paul Barnes. New York: Knopf, 1999.

Articles

Barry, Kathleen L. "Susan B. Anthony: Radical Egalitarian of Women's Rights." *Women Public Speakers in the United States, 1800–1925,* ed. Campbell, Karlyn Korhs. Westport, CT: Greenwood Press, 1993.

Dunbar, Olivia Howard. "Interview with Susan B. Anthony." *Leavenworth Weekly Times.* November 16, 1899. Copy in author files.

Erickson, Amy. "Mistress and Marriage." *History Workshop Journal,* Oxford University Press. Autumn 2014.

Bibliography

New York Tribune, Sunday, February 15, 1920, 70; chroniclingamerica.loc.gov/lccn/sn83030214/1920-09-29/ed-1/seq-1.

Wineapple, Brenda. "Ladies Last." *The American Scholar*, summer 2013. theamericanscholar.org/ladies-last/#.Wm9mc3eZOWY.

"Reshaping the Body: Clothing and Cultural Practice." University of Virginia, Historical Collections at the Claude Moore Health Sciences Library. exhibits.hsl.virginia.edu/clothes/19th_corset/.

Cases

Bradwell v. State of Illinois, 83 U.S. 130 (1873).

Minor v. Happerset, 88 U.S. 162 (1864).

Rhodes v. North Carolina, 61 N.C. 453 (1868).

Acknowledgments

I owe a very special thanks to Faye Dudden, Professor Emeritus of History at Colgate University, an expert in women's history in the nineteenth century, for kindly reading the manuscript for accuracy and providing generous comments and feedback. Any errors, of course, are my own. There is much myth and falsehood surrounding the story of Susan B. Anthony, particularly concerning the portions of Anthony's life that today are considered the most controversial—those involving George Francis Train. I couldn't have written this book, particularly those difficult chapters, without standing on the shoulders of such scholars as Kathleen Barry, Faye Dudden, and Ann D. Gordon, who painstakingly pieced together the historical record to offer an accurate chronology and to illuminate the facts and political maneuverings.

Special thanks, as always, to the entire Abrams team: Howard Reeves, editor beyond compare; the design team, including Sara Corbett, Siobhán Gallagher, and Chad Beckerman, who turns mere manuscripts into works of art; managing editor Amy Vreeland; Emily Daluga, who is such a pleasure to work with, and who holds together all the bits and pieces; Tom McNellis, Rob Sternitzky, and Regina Castillo, who make sure I follow the rules of English usage; and of course, as always, Andy.

Index

Note: Page numbers in *italics* refer to illustrations.

abolition, 46, 60
abolitionists
    Civil War blamed on, 103
    Douglass as, 116
    with Lincoln, 89
    Phillips as, 107
activism
    of Gage, F., 1
    against slavery, 1
    Stanton, E., with, 169
African Americans
    Civil War and, 101
    Friend's Meeting and, 28
    jobs for, 105–6
    right to vote for, 107, 117
American Anti-Slavery Society, 22, 121
    agent for, 70
    right to vote with, 108
    travel cost for, 73
American Woman Suffrage Association, 145, 173–74
Anthony, Daniel, 7, *104*
    attachment to, 19
    cotton industry with, 13
    death of, 32, 95
    finical crisis for, 23–24
    marriage of, 9
    with McLean, J., 14
    Read, L., and, 8
    on slaves, 15
Anthony, Daniel Jr., 12
Anthony, Eliza, 16–17
Anthony, Guelma, 10, 12, 22, 91, 161

Anthony, Hannah, 10, 12, 16, 33, 169
Anthony, Jacob Merritt, 16
Anthony, Mary, *179*, 186
Anthony, Susan B. *See specific topics*

Battenville, NY, 30
    home school in, 15
    leaving of, 18
    return to, 25
Baumfree, Isabella, 57
Bingham, John A., 154
birth home, *6*
Black Codes, 110, *111*
Blackwell, Henry, 128, 130, 145
Bloomer, Amelia, 50, 52, *54*, 55
bloomers, 54
Bradwell, Myra, 163

Canajoharie Academy, 34, 35, 46
Catt, Carrie Chapman, *175*
Celebration of the Abolition of Slavery in the District of Columbia, 92–93
Center Falls, 26–27
Civil War, 123, 171, 193
    abolitionists blamed for, 103
    African Americans and, 101
    Draft Act in, 99
    with Lincoln, 88
    slavery and, 89
Clay, Henry, 29
Cleveland, Grover, 187, *188*
Clinton, Hillary, 198

Index

Constitution
    Civil War and, 88
    slavery and, 78, 96
    Thirteenth Amendment in, 104, 110, 113, 117–18
Cowan, Edgar, 124

Davies, Charles, 64, 67, 75–76
Deborah Moulson's Female Seminary, 18
    departure from, 24
    Quaker liberalism in, 21
Declaration of Rights of the Women of the United States, 165–66
Declaration of Sentiments, 38, 55

Douglass, Frederick, 38, 46, *46*, 112, 116, 106, 122, 129-30, 136, 141-42, 143

Ellet, Elizabeth F., 82–83
Emancipation Proclamation, 94–96
Emerson, Ralph Waldo, 179
Equal Rights Association, 141, 144

Fair, Laura
    men protection for, 150
    murder case with, *149*, 151
family home, 10, 25
Ferry, Thomas W., 166
Fifteenth Amendment, 119, 135, 141-42, 144, 145, 146, *147*, 192, 195
Fillmore, Millard, 159
Fourteenth Amendment, 118, *153-154*, 154, 157, 162, 163
funeral, 191–92

Gage, Frances, 1–2, 157, 171
Gage, Matilda Joslyn, 168
Garrison, William Lloyd, 46, 55, 84, 89, 99, 106, 192
Gibbons, Abigail Hopper, 82
Grant, Ulysses S., 106, 156

Hale, Sarah, 68
Hardscrabble, 26
Harper, Frances Ellen Watkins, 123
Harper, Ida Husted, *180*
Hawley, Joseph R., 166
History of Woman Suffrage (Stanton, E., Anthony, S., and Gage, F.), 58, 169–70, *171*
home school, 15
Hyatt, Sally Ann, 15–16

industrial revolution, 31, 60
insane asylum, 79, *80–81*
integration, 75
International Council of Women, 171, 185, *186*

Jackson, Andrew, 23, 28
Jackson, Francis, 120

Keeney, Marshal E. J., 157

late life
    demeanor in, 186
    health during, 183
    illness in, 190
    men during, 189
    speaking tour during, 184
    of Stanton, E., 184–85

Index

law of coverture, 3–4
lectures, 170
    handbill for, *152*
    against slavery, 70
    tour with, 49, 69, 87
    on women's rights, 59, 68
Lee, Richard Henry, 166, *167*
liberals, 50–51
Lincoln, Abraham, 20, 77, 79, 88, 89, 94, 96

Manhood Suffrage, 135
marriage, 9
    anger from, 152
    contracts and loans in, 196
    problems of, 43
    property rights and, 177
    proposals of, 36
    widowers' proposal for, 33–34
    for women, 42
    women's rights and, 143–44
May, Samuel, 87
Mayo, A. D., 85
McClellan, George B., 102
McLean, Aaron, 27
McLean, John, 14
Memoirs Reminiscences (Stanton, E.), 80
Miller, Elizabeth Smith, 52
Minor, Virginia, *162*
"Miss Hangman for Sheriff," 141
"Miss" protocol, 31
Modern Persecutions or Insane Asylums Unveiled (Packard), 81
Mosher, Eugene, 33
Mott, Lucretia, *21*, 22, 37, 120, 141
Mott, Lydia, 79, 90

Moulson, Deborah, 22

National American Woman Suffrage Association, 174, 183, 193
National Woman Suffrage Association, 145, 162, 165, 173–74
National Women's Rights Convention, 59, 90, 114
Native Americans, 105
New Rochelle, NY, 27–28
New York City, 99, 101
New York State Teachers' Convention, 65
    integration speech at, 75
    speaking at, 66
    women's rights and, 67
Nineteenth Amendment, 196

Packard, Elizabeth Parsons Ware, 81
Phelps, Phoebe
    antislavery work and, 84
    committed to insane asylum, 79, *80*
    husband of, 82, 86
    sanity of, 83
Philadelphia Female Anti-Slavery Society, 22
Phillips, Wendell, 84, 106, *107*, 114, 115, 119, 130
politics
    entrance to, 43
    reformer for, 50
    shut out of, 196
portraits
    Anthony, D., *9*
    Anthony, S., *vi*, *63*, *178*
    Read, L., *9*

Index

"The Power of the Ballot," 150
property rights
    divorce and, 3
    law of coverture and, 3–4
    marriage and, 177
    men with, 125
    women and, 37
proslavery advocates
    against Anthony, S., 87
    mobs of, 87
    slavery and, 71, 77
    in Supreme Court, 96
Purvis, Robert, 120–22

Quakers (Friends), 7, 8, 28, 33
    dances for, 36
    in Deborah Moulson's Female Seminary, 21

Read, Joshua, 25, 32, 37
Read, Lucy, *9*, 32
    Anthony, D., and, 8
    death of, 170
    last dance of, 9
    mother of, 7
    unhappiness for, 13
Read, Margaret, 41
Reminiscences (Stanton, E.), 64
Remond, Charles Lenox, *121*
Revolution, 132, 134, 148
Rhodes, Elizabeth, 138
right to vote, 123
    for African Americans, 107, 117
    amendment for, 195
    with American Anti-Slavery Society, 108
    arrest with, 157
    under Fourteenth Amendment, 157
    National Woman Suffrage Association and, 162
    Phillips on, 119
    with Suffragist Parade, *194*
    Supreme Court and, 162
    trial for, 159–60
    "The Woman Who Dared," *158*
    for women, 108, 126
Rochester, NY
    move to, 32
    new family farm in, *33*
    return to, 46
Roosevelt, Theodore, 187, 189
Rose, Ernestine, 70
rule of thumb, 138–39

Sargent, Aaron, 169
school integration, 105
Second Reconstruction Act, 118
Selden, Henry R., 156
Senate Committee on Privileges and Elections, 169–70
Seneca Falls Convention, 37–38
Shaw, Anna
    friend of, 189, *190*
    tribute from, 192
slavery, 1, 14, 15, 47, 70, 72, 77, 78, 84–85, 89, 94, 96, 103, 112. *See also* proslavery advocates
speaking tour, 55, 99, 180
    during late life, 184
    "The Power of the Ballot," 149
Stanton, Elizabeth Cady, 55, *61*, 76, 80, 107, 110, *178*
    on babies, 91
    death of, 185
    Douglass on, 136, 143

Index

on Fifteenth Amendment, 119
friends with, 62
late life of, 184–85
making laws and, 164
meeting of, 60
on men, 135–37
on Phillips, 115
smear job on, 133
Stanton, Henry, 62
Stevens, Thaddeus, 114
Stone, Lucy, 122, *123*, 126, 145, 174
Suffragist Parade, *194*
Sumner, Charles, 101, 104, 117
Supreme Court, *147*
    Fourteenth Amendment and, 163
    proslavery advocates in, 96
    right to vote and, 162
    women in, 197

teaching
    for Anthony girls, 17
    at Canajoharie Academy, 35
    growing restless with, 41
    in New Rochelle, 27–28
    salary of, 25
    with women's education, 18
temperance movement, 40, 48
Thirteenth Amendment
The Times, 23
Train, George Francis, *128*, 129–30
Troy Female Seminary, 62
Truth, Sojourner, 57–58, 61, 120

Underground Railroad, 48
Union Army, 92, 102
Universal Suffrage, 116
upper-class girls, 20

Van Buren, Martin, 28–29
Vaughn, Hester, 138–40
Victoria (Queen), 171
A Vindication of the Rights of Woman (Wollstonecraft), 38, *39*

Whigs, 29
Willard, Emma, 62
Wilson, Woodrow, 193, 195
Wollstonecraft, Mary, 38
Woman's Journal, 148
women's colleges, 176–77
women's education
    with Quakers, 8
    teaching with, 18
Women's Movement, 197
Women's National Loyal League, 97–98, 101
women's oppression, 4
women's rights, 177
    abolition and, 60
    donations for, 74
    Fifteenth Amendment and, 142
    as human rights, 198
    at inns, 2–3
    lectures on, 59, 68
    marriage and, 143–44
    movement of, 114
    "new true woman" with, 69
    New York State Teachers' Convention and, 67
    Seneca Falls Convention for, 37
women's voting rights
    suffrage, *114*, 130, 171, 188
    voter registration, 155, 162
Woodhull, Victoria, 153

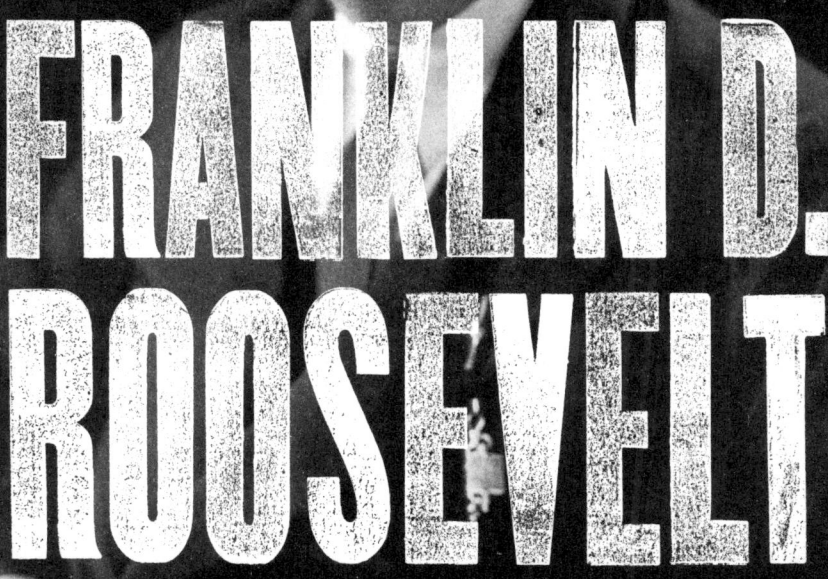

The next book in
The Making of America
★ *series* ★

FRANKLIN D. ROOSEVELT
The Making of America

★ TERI KANEFIELD ★
Abrams Books for Young Readers
New York

★ PROLOGUE ★

America Under Attack

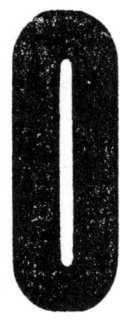n the morning of Sunday, December 7, 1941, at about 8:30, Franklin Delano Roosevelt, President of the United States, was in his private suite on the second floor of the White House, reading his newspapers as he waited for his valet to help him into his wheelchair. For twenty years—since an illness at the age of thirty-nine—he'd been paralyzed from the waist down.

As he waited, he flipped through the *New York Times*, the *Herald Tribune,* two Washington, D.C., papers, and even the *Chicago Herald,* a paper he despised. For the past two years, the

★ ★ ★ FRANKLIN D. ROOSEVELT ★ ★ ★

newspapers had been blaring ominous news: German tanks rolled into Poland! Nazi Germany conquered Belgium, Holland, and Luxembourg! The Nazis marched into Paris! German bombs were blitzing England! German tanks thundered into Moscow! Fascist Italy conquered Albania! Japan invaded Manchuria, China, and the oil production zones of Borneo and Central Java!

Now Japan and the United States were on the brink of war. The day before had brought alarming news when United States intelligence officers intercepted a fourteen-part message Japan had sent to its Western diplomat. At 3:00 p.m. the message had been sent to Washington, D.C., where intelligence officers set to work deciphering the code. Just before Roosevelt had gone to bed the night before, an officer had come to tell him that the first thirteen parts had been deciphered. They appeared to be a set of resolutions to the United States government detailing why negotiations had broken down.

That morning—as Roosevelt was reading his newspapers—intelligence officers across town were already at work, deciphering the final part. Within a few hours, they broke the code and learned that Japan planned to cut off diplomatic relations with the West at 1:00 p.m. on the East Coast, which would be 10:00 a.m. on the West Coast, and much earlier throughout the Pacific.

America Under Attack

The officers concluded that Japan was planning a morning attack on the United States. The problem was that nobody knew where. So Secretary of War Henry Stimson ordered warnings telegraphed to United States military bases throughout the Pacific, beginning with the most likely targets of Manila and Panama. He had trouble telegraphing warnings to Hawaii because radio contact was broken. After some delays, he sent the alert by commercial telegraph.

By the time his warning reached headquarters in Pearl Harbor on the Hawaiian island of Oahu, it was too late: Japanese fighter planes were roaring over Pearl Harbor, unleashing a torrent of bombs, catching the sleepy harbor by surprise. The devastating attack obliterated almost the entire American fleet and killed twenty-four hundred sailors, soldiers, and civilians. It was the most catastrophic foreign attack in American history.

✯ ✯ ✯ ✯ ✯ ✯ ✯ ✯ ✯ ✯ ✯ ✯ ✯ ✯ ✯

The USS *Arizona* as it appeared before the attack

★★★ FRANKLIN D. ROOSEVELT ★★★

Eleanor Roosevelt, the president's wife, was entertaining guests for lunch. The president joined the group, but after a short time, he excused himself and wheeled himself from the room. "I was disappointed but not surprised," Eleanor wrote later. "The fact that he carried so many secrets in his head made it necessary for him to watch everything he said, which in itself was exhausting."

Roosevelt and his friend and advisor Harry Hopkins had their lunch in private, in what was then called the Oval Study. After they finished eating, Hopkins stretched out on a couch and they made small talk.

The phone rang. When Roosevelt answered, the White House operator told him the caller was Colonel Frank Knox, secretary of the navy. "Put him on," Roosevelt said.

When Knox came to the line, his voice sounded choked. "Mr. President," he said. "It looks as if the Japanese have attacked Pearl Harbor."

"No!" Roosevelt gasped.

Soon the Oval Study was crowded with cabinet members, aides, and secretaries. Messengers rushed in and out with news. The phone rang almost constantly. All around was panic and hubbub—but Roosevelt had regained his composure. "Deadly

The USS *Arizona* during the attack

calm," was how Eleanor later described him. "His reaction to any great event was always to be calm," she said. "If it was something that was bad, he just became almost like an iceberg and there was never the slightest emotion that was allowed to show." He was so emotionless, in fact, that rumors later circulated that he knew in advance of the attack. Some even claimed he invited the attack as a way to solidify his own power and get America into the war. In fact, Roosevelt, while tightly controlled, was as surprised as everyone else.

He knew the Japanese attack meant that the United States would have to fight a war on two fronts: against Germany in Europe, and Japan in the East. He also knew that America was not prepared. "We haven't got the navy to fight in both the Atlantic and the Pacific," he told Eleanor. "So we will have to build up the navy and the Air Force and that will mean we have to take a good many defeats before we can have a victory."

✯ ✯ ✯ ✯ ✯ ✯ ✯ ✯ ✯ ✯ ✯ ✯ ✯ ✯

When President Roosevelt had trouble relaxing because he was beset with worries, he had a method for soothing himself. He would close his eyes and imagine himself a boy again at home in Hyde Park, New York, standing with his sled

America Under Attack

---

atop the hill that stretched to the wooded bluffs of the Hudson River. He remembered each twist and turn of the hill in such vivid detail that he could visualize himself maneuvering his sled around each obstacle. He imagined reaching the bottom, and then pulling the sled up the hill and zooming down again.

For a few blissful moments, he wasn't the president of the United States about to face a world war—and he wasn't paralyzed from the waist down. He was a carefree boy, home again, sledding on the banks of the Hudson River.

1
Always Bright and Happy

"All that is in me goes back to the Hudson."
— *Franklin Delano Roosevelt*

Franklin Delano Roosevelt was born into a world of ease and luxury. He lived with his parents in a fifteen-room mansion in the well-to-do village of Hyde Park, located about eighty-five miles up the Hudson River from New York City. The one-hundred-acre estate featured large stables, a track for his father's racehorses, and a garden house. Franklin had a half-brother, the child of his father's first marriage. His brother was named James for their father, but went by the nickname of Rosy. When Franklin was

Always Bright and Happy

Franklin Delano Roosevelt's birthplace in Hyde Park, New York

born, Rosy was twenty-eight years old, and married with a mansion of his own and two small children.

After Franklin was born, the doctors told his mother that she wouldn't be able to have any more children. As a result, she lavished all of her attention on Franklin. Wealthy nineteenth-century mothers generally delegated childcare duties to nurses and nannies, but Sara Delano Roosevelt insisted on caring for her own baby. Franklin's mother was thus the central figure of his early childhood. His father was the energetic companion who taught him to sled before he was two, and to skate, sail, ride a horse, and shoot a hunting rifle as soon as he was old enough. His passions were ships and the sea. "Even as a little mite," Sara said, "he declared himself a sea-faring man."

★ ★ ★ FRANKLIN D. ROOSEVELT ★ ★ ★

His father was easygoing. His mother was determined to mold her son into a gentleman, but she did so gently. Young Franklin thus knew nothing of harsh discipline, family quarrels, or anger.

"In thinking back to my earliest days," he said later, "I am impressed by the peacefulness and regularity of things both in respect to places and people." Whether at home in Hyde Park or another of his family residences, his routine was the same: Up at seven, breakfast at eight, lessons until eleven, lunch at noon, more lessons until four, two hours of play, then supper and bed. Franklin's playmates were chosen from among his parents' circle of friends, but Franklin spent most of his time with adults. His tutors, carefully handpicked by his mother, gave him lessons in Latin, French, German, penmanship, history, and arithmetic. During his family's extended stays in Europe, he attended school there and became fluent in both German and French.

One day when Franklin was about eight, Sara noticed that he seemed melancholy. She asked him if was unhappy. He thought for a moment, and then said, "Yes, I am unhappy."

She asked him why. He grew thoughtful. As Sara later told the story: "Then with a curious little gesture that combined entreaty with a suggestion of impatience, he clasped his hands in front of

Always Bright and Happy

him and exclaimed, 'Oh, for freedom.'" Sara gave the matter some thought, and talked it over with James. The next morning, she told Franklin he could do whatever he pleased that day. He didn't have to obey any of his usual rules and could "roam at will."

For a full day, she paid no attention to him. His tutors had a day off. That evening, he came back to the house muddy, tired, and hungry. "We could only deduce that his adventures had been a little lacking in glamour," Sara later explained, "for the next day, quite of his own accord, he went contentedly back to his routine."

Franklin with his father, James, 1887

Franklin with his mother, Sara, 1887

★★★ FRANKLIN D. ROOSEVELT ★★★

★ ★ ★ ★ ★ ★ ★ ★ ★ ★ ★ ★ ★

Franklin's roots went deep in American history. The first Roosevelt to come to America was Claes van Roosevelt, a Dutchman who landed in New Amsterdam (later renamed New York) in 1650. In time, the Roosevelts amassed a fortune in Manhattan real estate and the West Indian sugar trade. Franklin's great-great-grandfather Isaac Roosevelt worked with Alexander Hamilton to persuade the New York legislature to ratify the U.S. Constitution. Among James Roosevelt's close friends was George McClellan, the general who had led Union troops in the Civil War and who challenged Abraham Lincoln for the presidency in 1864.

★ ★ ★ ★ ★ ★ ★ ★ ★ ★ ★ ★ ★

Read on in the next installment of
THE MAKING OF AMERICA
series:

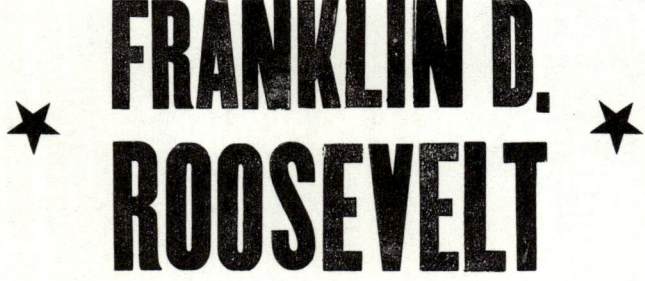

Read all of the
THE MAKING OF AMERICA
series

★ ★ ★ ★ ★ ★ ★ ★ ★ ★ ★ ★

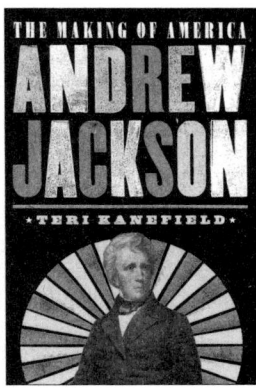

★ ★ ★ ★ ★ ★ ★ ★ ★ ★ ★ ★ ★ ★ ★

TERI KANEFIELD

is a lawyer and the author of *The Girl from the Tar Paper School, The Extraordinary Suzy Wright,* the Making of America series, and more. Her awards include the Jane Addams Book Award and the Carter G. Woodson Middle Book Level Award. She lives in San Luis Obispo, on the beautiful central California coast.

★ ★ ★ ★ ★ ★ ★ ★ ★ ★ ★ ★ ★ ★ ★